PRAISE FOR *AN OTHER KINGDOM*

Whenever Block, Brueggemann, and McKnight get together on the topic of community, the outcome is both inspirational and practical. That's been the case for years, and it's the case once again with this fine book. At a time when so many are being left behind by our culture of individualism, competition, and consumerism, this book—with its emphasis on remembering that we're all in this together and have gifts that can help meet others' needs—is a grounded call to compassion and justice.

> **Parker J. Palmer,** author of *Healing the Heart of Democracy, A Hidden Wholeness,* and *Let Your Life Speak*

Walter Brueggemann teams up with two veteran community organizers to not only astutely analyze our current North American context but also give us specific, practical ways we can move toward greater neighborliness for the common good. Hard-hitting judgment and joyful encouragement all in one book.

> **Will Willimon,** professor of Christian Ministry, Duke Divinity School, Durham, North Carolina, and United Methodist Bishop (ret.)

To change the conversation, it's necessary to understand what is wrong with the one we're currently having. Block, Brueggemann, and McKnight do just that. Original and illuminating. Prophetic and liberating!

> **Robert Inchausti,** author of *Thomas Merton's American Prophecy, Subversive Orthodoxy,* and *The Ignorant Perfection of Ordinary People*

These gentle men, the authors of this book, are "waiting for a social movement"—one that will of necessity restore our neighborhoods and our humanity. They intuit it. *An Other Kingdom: Departing the Consumer Culture* is a statement of their longing. The book is not sentimental. John McKnight, for one, is a trained Alinsky organizer. He knows the realities of Chicago's streets, of its notorious projects, of its vibrant churches, of its very democratic soul. But he's rather hopeful of fundamental economic, social, and cultural transformation, reminiscent of economist Fritz Schumacher.

"Our basic intent in writing this book is to shrink the market as the primary means of cultural identity, schools as source of learning, systems as the source of care, price as the measure of value, productivity as the basis for being." And so they have done. The movement they seek is waiting for us.

> **Susan Witt,** Schumacher Center for a New Economics

An Other Kingdom is not just for people of faith, it is a gift for anyone who seeks to understand how we can become better at being human together. Its authors are modern-day Magi. In place of gold, Peter, Walter, and John offer common wealth; in place of frankincense they offer mystery; and in place of myrrh they offer neighborliness. As the free market falls like a house of cards around our ears and the captains of industry draw our planet toward the precipice, this book offers sight of a sustainable and sustaining future.

> **Cormac Russell,** author of *Asset-Based Community Development: Looking Back to Look Forward,* managing director of Nurture Development, faculty member of ABCD Institute, and lead steward for ABCD in Europe

We've had enough End Times theology based on fear and revenge. It's time for an End-of-Our-Time theology based on faith, hope, and love. That's what *An Other Kingdom* provides. . . . Unlike many books that merely tell us how bad things are, leaving us anxious and depressed, these author-activists provide us with an alternative vision of a neighborly society, one that draws upon our deepest sacred and secular traditions and is already being constructed by ordinary people in many local communities.

> **Walter T. Davis,** professor (emeritus), San Francisco Seminary

Here begins the A-B-C of indigenous common sense in most cultures based on good relationships and shared meaning. An alternative culture detailed by Peter Block, Walter Brueggemann, and John McKnight is in actuality something extending from ancient patterns of survival. This (k)new language of covenant re-kindles trust and service to higher principles and helps us recognize each other again.

> **Manulani Aluli Meyer,** former associate professor of education at the University of Hawai'i at Hilo and world scholar-practitioner of Hawaiian and indigenous epistemology

For those who have that feeling deep inside them that something is seriously wrong with the reigning economy but cannot quite put their finger on it or cannot conceive of anything different replacing it, this book is crucial. . . . The language of this book is clear as it pushes us toward a different kind of life, a different way for life, and different conditions for living.

> **Olivia C. Saunders,** New Providence, The Bahamas

This is the work of three wise elders who have spent a lifetime of inquiry into the human good. . . . *An Other Kingdom* questions and provides alternatives to the dominant assumptions that guide our aspirations, our choices, and hence our lives. As long as these local and global narratives remain unexamined, they will continue to have the power to persuade us and our neighbors to act unknowingly against our best interests. The language within is beautifully economic and precise. It is best read slowly with reflection, as one would read poetry.

> **Ward Mailliard,** vice president and member of the executive board at Mount Madonna School, Watsonville, California

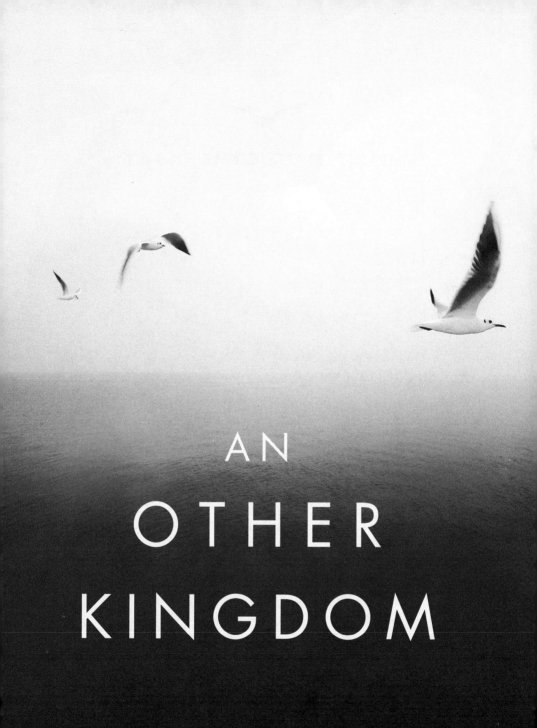

AN
OTHER
KINGDOM

SELECTED OTHER WORKS BY

PETER BLOCK

The Answer to How Is Yes
Community: The Structure of Belonging
Stewardship

WALTER BRUEGGEMANN

Journey to the Common Good
The Prophetic Imagination
Theology of the Old Testament

JOHN McKNIGHT

The Abundant Community, with Peter Block
Building Communities from the Inside Out, with John P. Kretzmann
The Careless Society: Community and Its Counterfeits

PETER WALTER JOHN
BLOCK BRUEGGEMANN McKNIGHT

AN
OTHER
KINGDOM

DEPARTING THE CONSUMER CULTURE

WILEY

For general information about our other products and services, please contact our Customer Care Department within the United States at (800) 762-2974, outside the United States at (317) 572-3993 or fax (317) 572-4002.

Wiley publishes in a variety of print and electronic formats and by print-on-demand. Some material included with standard print versions of this book may not be included in e-books or in print-on-demand. If this book refers to media such as a CD or DVD that is not included in the version you purchased, you may download this material at http://booksupport.wiley.com. For more information about Wiley products, visit www.wiley.com.

Library of Congress Cataloging-in-Publication Data has been applied for and is on file with the Library of Congress.
ISBN-13 978-1-119-19472-9 (pb);
ISBN 978-1-119-19473-6 (epdf);
ISBN 978-1-119-19474-3(epub)

Printed in the United States of America

10 9 8 7 6 5 4 3 2 1

To all those who have struggled to show us the way to an other kingdom.

CONTENTS

SIGNS OF THE TIMES   xiii

INTRODUCTION: Context Is Decisive   xvii

    The Landscape of the Market World   xx
    Enclosure   xxi
    Covenantal Versus Contractual Order   xxi
    The Neighborly Covenant   xxii

CHAPTER 1 The Free Market Consumer Ideology   1
    Scarcity   2
    Certainty and Perfection   3
    Privatization   3
    The Institutional Assumptions   4
        Better Management/Technology Is the Fix   4
        Interpersonal Is a Problem   5
        Competition Trumps Trust   5
    Toward a Neighborly Culture   6
    A Culture Based on Covenant   6

CHAPTER 2 Neighborly Beliefs   9
    Abundance   9
    Mystery   10
        Mystery at Work   11
        A Place for God   13
        Holiness   15
        Wilderness   15
    Fallibility   16

Failing to Be God   18
Grief   19
The Common Good   20

CHAPTER 3   Enough Is Enough: Limits of the Market Ideology   21
The Consumer Market Disciplines   22
Surplus   22
Predictability and Control   24
Speed and Convenience   26
The Sale of Convenience   26
Convenience Displaces Capacity   27
Digital Solutions   28
The Meaning of Money   29
Money and the Machine   30
Wishing for Safety, Believing in Growth   31
Competition and Class   32
Class by Design   33
Class Warfare and the Distribution of Wealth   34
The Myth of Individualism   36

CHAPTER 4   Tentacles of Empire   37
The Corporatization of Schools   38
No View from the Top   38
End of Aliveness   39
Mobility and Isolation   40
Un-Productive Wealth   41
Violence   42
Illusion of Reform   43

CHAPTER 5   The Common Good Is the New Frontier   45
The Neighborly Covenant   46
The Commons   48
An Alternative Social Order   49
Resisting the Empire   50
Off-Market Possibilities   51
The Neighborly Way   53

The Alternative to Restless Productivity   55
The Shadow Side of Community   58

CHAPTER 6   The Disciplines of Neighborliness   61
   Time   63
     A Time for All Things   63
     Time Is the Devil   63
     Standing in Line   65
     Kairos   65
   Food   66
     Food and Sacred Re-Performance   67
     The Local Food Movement   69
     Food and Culture   69
   Silence   71
     Listening   72
     Quakers and Time and Listening   72
     Sacraments of Silence   73
   Covenant: A Vow of Freedom and Faithfulness   74
     Covenant and Retributive Justice   75
   Abundance and the Right Use of Money   75
     Money and Our Affection for Place   77
   A Liturgy for the Common Good   77
     Prophetic Possibilities   78
     Story as Liturgy and Re-Performance   79
     The Re-Performing Power of Liturgy   79

POSTSCRIPT: Beyond Money and Consumption   81
   Timing Is Everything   82
   Signs of Change   83

COMMENTARIES   85
REFERENCES AND FURTHER READING   97
ACKNOWLEDGMENTS   103
ABOUT THE AUTHORS   105
INDEX   111

SIGNS OF THE TIMES

You know how to interpret the appearance of the sky, but you cannot interpret the signs of the times.

—Matt. 16:3

The intent of this book is to interpret certain signs of the times. These signs have to do with the need to depart the consumer market culture we have come to take for granted. This culture, with its constellations of empire and kingdom, produces endless conversations about climate warming, restoring the middle class in the northern economies, worldwide immigration driven by poverty, and political instability. We talk about financial bubbles, accessible health care, economic growth and contraction. We all want more companies to come to town, more factory jobs, more graduates in education, less crime and violence, everywhere. We seek more consumption and faster growth.

The premise of this book is that these conversations, generationally passed on as seemingly based on knowledge, science, and the assumption of progress, miss the signs of the times. All of these conversations are painfully predictable and at times despairing. They are symptoms of something more fundamental. Our belief is that the current programs, investments, or changes in political leadership will make modest improvements but little real difference. If we want to follow the signs of the times, we have to look at how our core economic beliefs have produced a culture that makes poverty, violence, ill health, and fragile economic systems seem inevitable.

Economic systems based on competition, scarcity, and acquisitiveness have become more than a question of economics; they have become the kingdom within which we dwell. That way of thinking invades our social order, our ways of being together, and what we value. It replicates the kingdom of ancient Egypt, Pharaoh's kingdom. It produces a consumer culture that centralizes wealth and power and leaves the rest wanting what the beneficiaries of the system have.

We invite you to a journey of departure from this consumer culture. We ask you to imagine an alternative set of economic beliefs that have the capacity to evoke a culture where poverty, violence, and shrinking well-being are not inevitable—a culture in which the social order produces enough for all. This, like reading fiction, requires a suspension of belief. Except in this case, what we take as true and inevitable is the fiction. This departure into another kingdom might be closer to the reality of our nature and what works best for our humanity. This other kingdom better speaks to the growing longing for an alternative culture, an alternative way of being together. We use the word *kingdom* in the title to remember the ancient stream we are drinking from. Kingdom, in its ambiguity, also speaks to both the sacred and the secular: sacred as in the Kingdom of God; secular as in the Chinese Middle Kingdom and the prevalence of kingdoms before the nation state was imagined and constructed in the nineteenth century.

We use the word *departing* to remember and re-perform the Israelites' Exodus into the wilderness away from Egypt, for the journey into a social order not based on consumption seems equally imposing.

Luckily, the exodus from a consumer, globalized culture into a neighborly, localized communal and cooperative culture has begun. We join the chorus of other agents of the alternative economy: food hubs, cooperative and social enterprises, the climate change activists, health activists, plus beacons of light like *Yes* magazine, the Democracy Collaborative, the Schumacher Center for a New Economics, Mondragon, and the Happiness streams emanating from the Dali Lama, Bhutan, economists like Mark Anielski, and architects like Christopher Alexander and Ross Chapin.

Our intent is to give name and visibility to these signs of the times, to add a small thread in solidarity with the un-credentialed voices and uncollateralized entrepreneurs who are rewriting our economic and communal narrative.

A cautionary note: We have written this departure narrative as a slow spiraling dialogue around a core set of ideas. We keep coming back to the dominant consumer culture story and the alternative neighborly culture story, hoping to add depth and nuance to the central point, in much the same way that we relish slow food, walkable distances, and time to reflect.

INTRODUCTION: CONTEXT IS DECISIVE

L et us begin by describing the nature of the consumer kingdom. We live within a dominant cultural narrative best described as the Free Market Consumer Ideology. This is a totalizing narrative, which provides the water within which most of our ideas and actions swim. The time is right to change the water and thereby the kingdom that it nourishes.

The Free Market Consumer Ideology is an economic narrative in which:

Free means that there should be few constraints on individuals and institutions. It signifies the elevation of individual rights. The freedom to do business and to privatize the common assets such as government, air, water and the land, as it suits us. This appropriated language of economic freedom is welded to the idea of democracy.

Market means that how we conduct commerce is a first priority. It is not just a place of buying and selling, it is a world view. An invisible hand, perhaps an instrument of God. It is touted as the essential element of democracy. If it must be protected by military action at home and abroad, which it does, then so be it.

Consumer means that our capacity to purchase is the measure of our well-being and our identity. That what is essential to life—such as raising children, our health, our safety, our care— can be outsourced and purchased. It also means that whatever we have is not enough.

Ideology means that our beliefs about Free, about Market, and about Consumer are True. Beyond question. Expressions of our real nature.

These are much more than a set of beliefs about an economy. These consumer market concepts shape and commodify the social order. They define our culture. This narrative is the lens through which we raise our children, tell the news, create our livelihood, label who is in and out, distribute empire, and define how we live. It identifies what really matters in the end and establishes the nature of our social relationships. It is the final word—the bottom line, to use its own terminology.

This book is an invitation to imagine social relationships ordered differently. Social relationships ordered around an alternative narrative that is founded on the ideas of neighborliness and covenant. A social order not based on the conception of consumption and contract.

Neighborliness means that our well-being and what really matters is close at hand and can be locally constructed or produced. In this modern time, neighborliness is considered quaint and nostalgic. To make neighborliness the center of our social order requires an act of imagination. It is counter-cultural. It is also a form of social interaction that is built on a covenant that serves the common good.

In order to imagine a mode of social interaction that serves the commons, we must become aware of the way social relationships are dominantly ordered among us now. It is difficult to see what we are swimming in. It is hard to imagine there is an alternative to what we consider to be true and inevitable.

Understanding the current social order is important because the cultural narrative is decisive. It has the power of context. It decides who has access to social power and social goods, and how people who are not deciders relate to the ones who do decide. The consumer and market authority we live within violates neighborly relations by stratifying social power according to money and its attendants—privilege, competition, self-interest, entitlement, surplus. The dominant modes of current social relationships fend off neighborliness at all costs, and at great cost.

The market ideology says that neighborly relationships are no longer required. That we are best ordered by commercializing all we can. That what we needed from neighbors can be obtained anywhere. The tools for livelihood have been stolen and replaced by the machines of contract. In this a culture is lost, superseded by the new reality. The major early step toward the modern cultural reality was "enclosure," the privatizing of the common land. Now we offshore in the name of globalization and outsource in the name of market efficiency. Every human endeavor is monetized. We now work for a living. In the move to industrialization, and the move to the cities, we left our local culture behind. The family became dependent on adult earnings outside a local culture, and we became laborers, wage earners. When we human beings are called laborer, wage earner, bread winner, it impacts our souls. Until industrialization came along, the concept of labor did not exist. Being paid based on the number of hours worked was inconceivable. When a person's effort was converted to wage earner, a person became an object. An object of cost and efficiency, an asset.

We moved away from the neighbor as a source of culture, memory, sense of place, and livelihood. We made subsistence living a problem to be solved. The casualty was the loss of a sense of the commons. What is at stake in the renewal of neighborliness is the restoration of the commons. The free market consumer ideology has produced a social disorder; people are no longer embedded in a culture that serves the common wealth, the common good.

Where we are headed in this book is to further the belief that to seek neighborliness and the common good means a shift in narrative. It is about reframing how we take our communal identity. Here we are proposing to identify what has been considered sacred language and use it as an opening into the experience of community and the commons. We are trying to lay out a faith narrative without the negative traces of sectarianism:

Faith as the assurance of things hoped for, the conviction of things not seen.

—Hebrews 11.1

This alternative narrative is not about the church, or religion, or certain values; these are at the center of the dominant current narrative, in which they become an argument. This faith narrative is about language and its transformative power.

The sacred language includes the words of covenant, vow, liturgy, re-performance, silence, mystery, and fallibility. This language and the experience it provokes become an alternative to the current dominant ideology from which we take our identity as a western culture, which is from the free market consumer society's affection for contract, scarcity, entertainment, newness, certainty, perfection, privatization, and the primacy of individual rights and interests.

THE LANDSCAPE OF THE MARKET WORLD

As a quick view of the landscape of the market and consumer world, we begin with a brief history of the free market consumer ideology:

Early Days	Eve becomes the first consumer. She follows the advice of the serpent, the first consultant. Eve picks the low-hanging fruit.
1582	Pope Gregory XIII refines the calendar. We lose eleven days in the process. We gain agreement on common dates for shipping, arrivals, and departures.
1607	Privatization of commons intensifies as James I enforces enclosure in Britain.
1776	Adam Smith writes in *The Wealth of Nations* that only the self-interest of the butcher will get your meat cut.
1843	Standard length of an inch established.
1847	Railway Clearing House in Great Britain adopts Greenwich Mean Time.
1949	President Harry S Truman declares in 1949 Inaugural Address that much of the world of the south and far-east suffers from underdevelopment. This came as a surprise to them.
1970	Milton Friedman declares in a *Time* magazine article that the sole purpose of business is to generate profit for shareholders. Any social purpose would be spending shareholder money and turn executives into civil servants.
2001	President George W. Bush urges the American people to go shopping as a response to 9/11.
2014	The Dow Jones Industrial Average closes above 18,000 for the first time, a comforting sign that the system is working.

ENCLOSURE

Enclosure is a place to start to deconstruct the free market narrative. Before the enclosure movement began, there were, in the British Isles and elsewhere, extensive public lands. Lands on which local residents could create a life and a livelihood. Common land on which to fish, farm, hunt, and be housed. Enclosure, actively begun in the sixteenth century and reinforced by James I, fenced in the public lands and made them private. There were protests and battles over the years, but after a couple of hundred years, virtually all the public lands went into private ownership. The landless working class became "labor" to service the machine, and the land went to feeding sheep. More profitable than feeding people.

The end result was a culture ordered by private interests. Commerce became married to king. What was produced was a culture that abandoned subsistence living and the values of local economy; it became a market devoted to scale, speed, and cost. A market that sanctified buying and selling. A culture where place, history, and tradition became irrelevant. A market culture based on contracts and void of covenantal relationships.

COVENANTAL VERSUS CONTRACTUAL ORDER

The language of covenant speaks to a market built on neighborliness, kinship, and common ownership. These are the cornerstones of the neighborly economy. An other kingdom. A covenantal relationship is based on a vow. It requires an act of imagination about neighborliness. You cannot point to covenant. You can only point to specific performances of covenant. Generosity, for example, is a specific performance of covenant. We are most familiar with the marriage vow. This is in our terms an act of neighborliness in which we choose to expend ourselves in care for someone who has no claim except personal needs and being in relationship. It is an act of fidelity that we could easily have avoided. We do not have to make that vow. Yet we felt summoned in some way to do it.

The modern consumer market economy is based on contract rather than covenant. A contractual relationship is based on a specific exchange of interests. It has a date and a dollar sign and a specific balanced exchange. For example, if you say I promise to give you $10.00, that's not a contract because nothing is specified in return. A contract is also time limited, it has a date. If I give you $10.00 and you promise to return it to me, it still is not a contract until you specify when you will pay it back. A covenant, by contrast, is free of specifics, free of date, and free of something in return.

When the public good is replaced with concern for private rights, we substitute a contract for what was covenant. When this happens we become ordered for scarcity instead of abundance. Time is contracted and we become concerned about speed. Certainty replaces mystery. Perfection substitutes for fallibility. Individual rights trump the common good, the common wealth.

A covenant is not without its risks. It demands reciprocity over time and violating it has its consequences: for example, loss of trust and consequent isolation. Covenant is a different way of ordering social relationships. It leads to a more intimate, a more interdependent way of being. Contracts are more based on agreement between autonomous individuals.

THE NEIGHBORLY COVENANT

Our task is to imagine a culture ordered differently. Imagine the human benefit of an alternative to the market ideology that defines our culture. We call this the Neighborly Covenant because it enlivens and humanizes the social order.

The Neighborly Covenant is an alternative to a market ideology that has reached its limits, no matter how high the Dow Jones Industrial Average climbs. The map we have really isn't working. It is visibly flawed. We see in every political campaign a rhetoric designed solely for marketing the candidate, not for meaning. We force all politicians into promising what they can't deliver. It becomes a concentrated version of the consumer ideology. Citizen as consumer, candidate as supplier. And so we campaign and vote on marketing slogans: liberal, conservative, values, democracy, end poverty, maintain standard of living, jobs, education, marriage this, guns that. These catchphrases are just code words, like advertising, that exploit people's needs and anxiety for the sake of candidate market share, namely winning their votes. This language is another subversion of the common good and the longing for public servants. We think the wish for an alternative culture will be fulfilled in the ballot box.

What we are proposing is language for alternative ways to a covenantal culture. The free market consumer ideology has defined the dominant codes, that particular way of talking about our culture. This is what has led us to stalemate. Our work is to create another set of code words— ones that are active beyond election years and have different substance in defining our communal identity. This is the departure. But first we want to be even clearer about what we are departing from.

1

THE FREE MARKET CONSUMER IDEOLOGY

I will pull down my barns and build bigger barns.

—Luke 12:18

The free market consumer ideology rests on four pillars: Scarcity, Certainty, Perfection, and Privatization. We take as true and inevitable that the contracts of commerce, resting on these pillars, which produce the commercial order, are the defining producer of our cultural order.

The culture produced by the free market consumer ideology relies on the idea of needs—real or manufactured—that can only be satisfied by production, distribution, and purchase. Monopoly is the unstated intention. It stands on autonomy as an organizing principle of culture; it is indifferent to gifts. When the apostle Paul asks, "What do you have that you have not been given?" the neighborly culture would say that everything I have has been given. The free market consumer ideology declares that everything I have I've earned.

This contract culture sends us down a track laid down by systems. In the systems world, whatever is un-organized and un-managed does not exist. Institutions are its structure of preference, and the "free" market a core conviction. Its idea of free is the absence of limits and restraints. There should be no restraints when it comes to production, distribution, or creating a compelling reason to purchase.

This reliance on needs, autonomy, and "free" supports the market's core beliefs in scarcity, certainty, perfection, and privatization.

SCARCITY

If I speak in the tongues of mortals and of angels but do not have love, I am a noisy gong or clanging cymbal. And if I have prophetic powers, and understand all mysteries and all knowledge, and if I have all faith, so as to remove mountains, but do not have love, I am nothing.
—I Cor. 13:1–2

Foundational to a culture ordered by contract is the question of whether there is enough to go around. Market and contract value only what is scarce.

If we construct an economy where quantities are controlled, based on the belief there is never enough for all, then we must compete to determine the winners. We begin this with grades in the first grade. There is the presumption that competition is essential and so there must be a normal distribution of grades. All students cannot receive high marks. If I get an A, someone in the class must perform poorly. It is an early lesson in how the marketplace ideology works. In a community organized around abundance, competition will occur, but it is not built into the system as a core design element. In a neighborly culture, the abundance of resources becomes the design element.

Scarcity is the deep belief that no matter how much we have, it is not enough. Therefore, more scale and growth is always required. Grow or die. The system of scarcity feeds on itself. We deny the abundance of the wilderness. This is the argument for free market consumption. This is what produces or manufactures scarcity. There is enough food to feed the world, but if the food were simply fully distributed, the market for food, as we know it, would collapse.

Both scarcity and abundance breed more of themselves. The practice of abundance is itself generative of more abundance. Agri-business is the practice of scarcity; it's like a cancer cell, which grows and grows until it destroys its host. Scarcity has the effect of destroying the host, the planet, and its ecology. Good farming is the practice of abundance. The soil becomes richer. It causes the land to generate more food for the neighborhood.

It isn't just that there is enough, but the practice of a belief in abundance makes more available. Theologically, what that means is if you practice abundance, God gives more.

Love has the same effect. It produces more of itself.

There is a conservative psychologist in Abilene, Texas, who talks about how leprosy is treated in the Bible: You don't want to touch someone with leprosy because you will get the disease. What he says is that Jesus touched lepers, but the process worked the other way: His health was transferred to the leper rather than leprosy being transferred to Him.

CERTAINTY AND PERFECTION

The free market consumer ideology promises a world of predictability and safety. It is repulsed by surprise and believes that all things are eventually knowable.

It believes in the limitless possibility of development and growth. You must strive for perfection, "failure is not an option." This applies to individuals, enterprises, and countries. Individuals are always a work in progress, enterprises grow or die, poor countries need to be developed by rich countries. Death is simply a medical failing, correctable over time. Human suffering is solvable by better and more services. Planetary risks will be solved by technology. Promoting and ensuring progress is the priority.

PRIVATIZATION

No Ammonite or Moabite shall be admitted to the assembly of the Lord.

—Deut. 23:3

The free market system is addicted to privatization. If it is a not-for-profit, if it's government, if it's schools, we have to make it more like a business. And so we have been privatizing for about 250 years, which means we have diverted resources from the common good and put them into the private sector.

The privatization that began with British enclosure was a violation of community. It was the removal of the rights of the commoners to use the land. The overthrow of the common good. And the covenant we have with each other.

THE INSTITUTIONAL ASSUMPTIONS

These four ideas—scarcity, certainty, perfection, and privatization—lead to ways of thinking we call the institutional assumptions. That means that I see my being, my future, the future I want to travel as one where the road is laid by the great institutions of society. If they are working, then I'm moving right down the highway. If they aren't working, then they need to be fixed with a bigger road-laying machine.

BETTER MANAGEMENT/TECHNOLOGY IS THE FIX

The fix for broken institutions is usually thought of in terms of questions of management or technology: How can we better manage this big machine, or what new technological invention can we bring to it that will make it finally lay the right road for me? This way of thinking rests on the premise that if we really compete and perform effectively, the cream will rise to the top. We will have the best technology and the best management at the top, and then down the highway we go. The market ideology has a near-religious trust in management and efficiency and a good interstate highway system.

The institutions that now provide the road are not just the institutions of commerce; they include those we call not-for-profits: the health and welfare institutions and the institutions of government. We hold the mechanistic idea in most all of our solutions that we have to fix the institutions. Individuals and the community are relegated to wait for the institutional fix. We simply play our part as members of the institution.

That machine cannot be fixed. It has done all it can do. And wherever we are going to go, it's a path that is constructive, not additive. We are going to have to re-conceive the nature of departure.

INTERPERSONAL IS A PROBLEM

A key tenet of institutions is that anything that is personal is a problem to be solved. Also, all things interpersonal are likewise problems to be solved. This is the beauty of automation. This thinking is basically about depersonalizing relationships. Institutions hold that we are not dependent on the unique characteristics of a small group of people. They care most about continuity, replication, and management. Everyone is dispensable.

When institutions talk about "going to scale" it means moving away from personal relationships. The very heart of institutionalization is to deny the value of unique human beings interacting together in productive ways and to replace this with a machine or digital account. It's the move from the tribe to the dynamo. And, in a sense, that is the track that western civilization has taken: the move from community to mechanistic institutionalization. We have bought the story that this is progress. Now we are looking for a path away from the notion that market success is progress.

COMPETITION TRUMPS TRUST

A culture of contest and contract regards everyone else as a competitor or a rival or a threat. So you never trust. It is a world that values dominance. A culture of covenant and neighborliness depends on trust. All the research and political theory about associational life says its base is trust. Money does not hold it together. The currency of contracts is money. The currency of covenant is trust.

The neighborly covenant replaces contracts with vows, which are simply unspecified promises. We have to decide whether we will trust a person's vow. If someone breaks a vow, there is no legal recourse as there is in a contract. When the Amish sold land, they wrote out the title deed, and the seller kept the document. The buyer, who normally takes possession of the deed, would hand it to the seller and say, "Well, why don't you keep that, so it'll remind you."

Trust is the glue of a communal narrative. It is a given, the absolute without which all the rest doesn't work. If employees have trust in an employer, then they know that they are not a displaceable part, but a member of the organization, the community. When that is not so, trust has all but disappeared.

TOWARD A NEIGHBORLY CULTURE

You shall love your neighbor as yourself.

—Lev. 19:18

There is no need to construct a world where we have to choose between systems and the communal path. There are limitations to localism, just as there are benefits to systems. The point is to overcome our isolation . . . to discover a way where we begin to have affection for the land and the commons.

We know we can't raise our children on our own. Even if we choose to home school our children, this won't work for all. We need schools. We just have to stop asking the school to raise our children. We want to re-formulate the systems we need to support the neighborly culture, not reform the ones we already have. We want to construct a communal world, one in which the functions that systems perform are congruent with what the community needs. When communities are fully functioning, when they are doing all the things they can do themselves, then we can re-discover what systems we need and what for.

We might ask then: What would a system look like that built neighborliness and covenantal relationships? It could begin with the question of how a human services system can create for its own workers the same cultural experience that it is intending to bring into the world. This would enable systems to support the kind of communal culture we are exploring.

A CULTURE BASED ON COVENANT

The alternative to the free market consumer culture is a set of covenants that supports neighborly disciplines, rather than market disciplines, as a producer of culture. These non-market disciplines have to do with the common good and abundance as opposed to self-interest and scarcity. This neighborly culture is held together by its depth of relatedness, its capacity to hold mystery, its willingness to stretch time and endure silence. It affirms its patience with fallibility, its appreciation of the value of re-performing aspects of a subsistence culture. For example, it calls for the right use of money, a willingness to eat food slowly, in season—food that is unprocessed and produced nearby.

This world stands in stark contrast to the dominant contractual and consumer culture that pivots around autonomy, independence, isolation, and a longing for certainty—and is always in a hurry. It is a shift away from a culture impatient with faith not based on reason, and wary of fidelity without recent results. Suppose I have done nothing for you lately?

The market culture has witnessed the disappearance of the neighborhood; it has seen neighborly relations bested by automatic garage door openers and the rise of the convenience store. I no longer need to borrow sugar; I can purchase it 24/7. This takes us to a different kingdom: neighborliness.

2

NEIGHBORLY BELIEFS

The neighborly Covenant rests on beliefs in Abundance, Mystery, Fallibility, and the Common Good. It places faith in our communal capacity versus our consumer capacity.

ABUNDANCE

To believe in abundance is to believe that we have enough . . . Even in the wilderness of an uncertain future. This thinking is a stretch of the imagination. It envisions social relationships in a different world, in a manna-based culture. It's a sharp contrast to a culture organized around commerce, a market ideology built on scarcity and the central premise that we cannot believe in sufficiency. It declares that we can never be satisfied with what we have, with the effect that customer satisfaction is truly an oxymoron.

A neighborly culture would declare that nature no longer needs to be productive. That raw land does not need to be developed. That we have enough without more development. It sees no need to extract from our lands and waters. It calls for an end to the belief that a community or an institution or even business has to grow or die to survive and have a meaningful life. Believing in enough means we can stop identifying with progress as the path to the good life.

MYSTERY

It is the glory of God to conceal things, but the glory of kings to search it out.

—Prov. 25:2

The Neighborly Covenant promises an unknowable world. It is organized for surprise and believes that much of life is permanently unknowable. It values the vow, which is a commitment in the absence of specificity.

Mystery is not a problem to be solved. Mystery is an opening to the unknown. Liturgy and sacraments are a way of making mystery concrete—in Jewish tradition they are the path, the way of the Torah.

Acceptance of mystery opens the door to a set of communal disciplines such as time, food, silence, and re-performance. These disciplines lead us on a path that begins and ends in mystery. Believing in mystery is the initial act of departure, the doorway to an alternative future. It's an opening to creativity and imagination. It opens the door to a neighborhood or community organized by covenant.

What we are seeking is a gateway to the qualities that architect Christopher Alexander (1977) calls wholeness and aliveness. In trying to make sense of architecture in the 1970s, Alexander explored the reasons that when you walk into certain physical spaces your experience is different from what you sense in other spaces. He named this a "quality of aliveness." The purpose of architecture, in his view, is to create a physical built environment that conveys a sense of wholeness and evokes a quality of aliveness. He also concludes that this quality of aliveness cannot be defined. It can be produced by a knowledge of a pattern language, but not defined. Mystery then is essential to aliveness. Covenant is the expression of this connection; it is an act that evokes aliveness and draws out those qualities.

Philosopher and social critic Ivan Illich (1973) also speaks to aliveness in his book *Tools for Conviviality*. This book was a guidepost to a culture that chooses life, a culture that prizes tools developed and maintained by a community of users—tools for life, not a system of death. Illich sought a name for that portion of social life that had been, remained, or might become immune to the logic of economization (Cayley, 2015).

MYSTERY AT WORK

Theologically speaking, mystery, then, is a combination of surprise and aliveness. The theological tradition would say that mystery is occupied by the bottomless combination of fidelity and freedom, qualities that evoke the presence of God. A combination of fidelity and freedom has popularly been translated into the message that love wins. Rob Bell had an Evangelical mega-church until he wrote a book called *Love Wins* (2011). He was run out for promoting that message. The issue was that if love wins there is no moral binding, and you can't threaten people to act right. There's no retributive capacity, no market discipline to confine or make demands on us.

We see an inherent longing and readiness for community all around us. It is the bottomless combination of fidelity and freedom that funds our yearning. In other words, our yearning for community is not something we invented; it is innate, a given. This means that mystery is more than just unknown space; it is also an active agency. Mystery has work to do. An example is that famous scene the night after Martin Luther King, Jr.'s house was bombed in Montgomery. MLK was sitting at the kitchen table when he heard a voice say, "Martin, don't be afraid." Dr. King said he was never afraid again. Was that an act of daring imagination on his part, or a mystery? We say it was an active mystery that came to him and he chose to receive it.

There is always something that cannot be explained. And the best of the scientists know that. They don't claim any sovereignty over knowledge. Especially near the end of their careers, they acknowledge the unknowability or limitless nature of what they spent their lives pursuing.

The child knows mystery also. All children at some moment ask the question of where something comes from, where they come from. You can answer in every way imaginable, but the only response that satisfies is, "From God." This ends the questioning in a comforting way, so that something is no longer missing for them. It is simply unknowable. There is no place beyond reason, or confusion, or understanding, only the place of mystery.

Mystery also has a relationship to justice. Justice begins with a vow, a vow constituted of freedom and fidelity. This vow enables the emergence of justice. The wedding vow, again, has to do with the practice of freedom and fidelity that, when rightly done, will eventuate as justice for your partner. If you knew what was coming, it wouldn't be a vow; it would be a contract. A vow requires mystery to be valid and trustworthy.

Mystery creates space for surprise, in contrast to the market that places such a premium on certainty. Holiday Inn was the first big motel system. The alternative was tourist homes and little places that might or might not be very good places to stay . . . you never knew. Holiday Inn made a promise to its guests; when you walked in to your room, there would be a sign on the chest of drawers that said, "Holiday Inn. No Surprises."

The free market consumer culture hates uncertainty. In the corporate world your stock price does not really suffer too much if profits are down. What is intolerable is not predicting the decline or not predicting it accurately. If you predicted a 20 percent reduction and profits fall 5 percent, you are faulted for that. If you predict a 20 percent increase in sales and you have a 60 percent increase in sales, you are faulted for that, too. The investment community, perhaps the greatest disciple of certainty, thinks that you are not in control because you missed your projections by so much. It's called risk management. The consumer culture transposes mystery into ignorance in the belief that what is ignorant can be known and then controlled.

On Christmas Day 1939 King George VI gives an address just months after the beginning of WWII, and it looks like pretty dark days ahead for Britain. He ends his speech with a quotation from a popular poem, which reaches the British public in ways that not even Churchill had achieved:

> *And I said to the man who stood at the gate of the year:*
> *"Give me a light that I may tread safely into the unknown."*
> *And he replied: "Go out into the darkness and put your hand into the*
> *Hand of God.*
> *That shall be to you better than light and safer than a known way."*
> —Haskins, 1908

Like King George and the British in the early days of the Second World War, every community in its culture and its spiritual life has historically understood there were mysteries and had a take on them other than "How can we overcome what we do not know?" They viewed mystery as a wondrous thing. It provided a cosmology, a relationship with nature, the planets, and the stars, and a connection to all living things. These are the ways that people have understood mystery held in community. Mystery is the embodiment of spiritual life. So whenever we declare that we will advance civilization when we know more, we are choosing a place for certainty that it does not deserve.

A PLACE FOR GOD

In the pride of their countenance the wicked say, "God will not seek it out"; all their thoughts are, "There is no God."
—Psalm 10:4

Does God need to be part of the conversation about neighborliness and the common good? The sacred textural tradition calls for this. The claim of God stands as a limit against the reduction of reality to commodity, however one articulates that. That's the barrier. And that's the usefulness of God.

In the Hebrew Bible, God is a mystery who comes with a narrative. So He never characteristically says, "I am the Lord," but says, "I am the Lord that brought you out of the land of Egypt," out of the house of commodities. You don't get this God without this narrative. And then the liturgy becomes the re-performance of the narrative in which God is an embedded character.

One of the things that has always been helpful in my life, because I do believe in God, is in response to when people will say, "Tell me about God." And immediately I think, God is a mystery.

And so if I value mystery in life, then God becomes very important to me. It helps me in some ways toward a path of humility, peacefulness, rather than imperialness, and to understand that I do not and will not ever understand or command this place.

—Walter

In the world of religion, the mantra often heard is, "I'm spiritual, but not religious," which means "I belong to no community of accountability and I'm not rooted in any tradition. It's just me." Of course the covenantal way of thinking and being welcomes this stance. But it is also a sign of the times, an earmark of the culture: Spirituality becomes just one more example of the individual as the key unit. The collectiveness has been taken out of the "spiritual" experience. Autonomy reigns.

When you talk of God in public or civic spaces, you do so at a risk. The risk is excluding those who don't believe in a God or higher power. Take the woman who said, "You lost me when you mentioned the word *God*. I'm very spiritual, but not a believer." This, too, was an expression of individualism. Allowing that statement to come into the conversation builds community and trust; it makes the discussion of covenant and vows and fallibility even more authentic. It is also a sign that so much God-talk in our culture carries unintended baggage, born of the experience of many that the church became an instrument of certainty and control rather than mystery and freedom. That the church is an ideology that is a given. In this way, God has been made subordinate to the market.

Still, there needs to be space for a God conversation to hold up the mystery and silence that departing the consumer culture requires. Dostoyevsky (1880) famously said that without God everything is possible, but if God be there, some things are not possible. Science says that everything is possible. Mystery says there are things we don't know, and therefore things not possible.

The Tree of Knowledge in Genesis 3 is an attempt to penetrate the Holy Mystery of God. The story is about the idea of overreaching God's space. So is the text in Deuteronomy 8 where Moses speaks to coming into the good land of houses that you did not build: *Do not say the might of my hand has gotten me this wealth.* This indicates the view that it is all God's gift and to claim that what we have is from our effort alone is overreaching. The market world seeks immortality and perfection. An extreme example is the wealthy person who puts all his money into overcoming death. Who says, "I hate death."

The Genesis, Deuteronomy, and death-defying wealthy man examples are all about overreaching God's space. Contract is the hope for limitless growth. Covenant is the act of not overreaching. Relating neighbor to neighbor is not overreaching in your neighbor's space. It recognizes limits. The Tenth Commandant is to not covet.

HOLINESS

Holiness is the depth of mystery. What you can see in some of the parts of the texts like Leviticus is that they try to administer holiness. They made rules for the sake of control. But holiness is the Hebrew Bible's attempt to talk about mystery. If you try to define the word *holy*, you can't do it. It's a mystery. It's beyond that limit. It's like God.

The point is, we are associating community building with holiness. Community is the reconstruction of individual well-being through the well-being of the whole. This is very different from beginning with individual self-interest and believing that the invisible hand of the market will create communal well-being. How do you reduce suffering in the world? We say you do it by building community; and in trying to give form to the landscape of community, we are asking you to take a spiritual path.

We recognize that there is not much precision in any discussion of mystery. What we can say is that every neighbor is somehow a carrier or reflector of holiness and therefore must be honored in some way and not just utilized. The holiness of God in the biblical tradition is then transposed into the awesomeness of the neighbor.

Community is people wrapped in a mystery. Community understands through their story, which gives shape and meaning to the mystery. Story honors our common experience.

WILDERNESS

The wilderness is the Old Testament metaphor for a covenantal social order. The Exodus narrative tells the story about Israel's leaving Pharaoh's Egypt. The Israelites went into the wilderness, a place where there were no viable life support systems. Its only virtue was that it was beyond the reach of Pharaoh. What they discovered, according to the narrative, is that when they went into this desolate place, it turned out to have the life supports of bread as manna, water from rock, and meat from quail. It turned out that the wilderness was presided over by the gift-and-life-giving God. In our terms it would be a covenantal, unspecified place of neighborliness.

The neighborhood and neighborliness are the unexplored modern wilderness. When viewed through the lens of the market, our neighborhoods would be assumed to be not viable because they do not have enough resources. There are no managed structures for consumption. What has never disappeared, though, is the manna of the modern wilderness: the gifts and the capacities and the teachables of your neighbors. The story of an alternative social order is that we can discover in the local world that there are places where we can go that we once thought had nothing that we need.

The analog in our time for being beyond Pharaoh's reach is being beyond the reach of financial credit systems, payday loan operators, developers, the bureaucracy, all the imperial institutions. The communal path into a neighborly culture can be considered a step into the wilderness, with its uncertainty and lack of visible means of support. The consumer culture, however, is so embedded in our habits and brain wiring that when we move toward the wilderness of covenant and mystery, we are always drawn back to a world of control and contract.

The wilderness is an unattractive proposition for a culture fearful of strangers and immigrants, one that does not welcome the Other into it. Even a group that started as an authentic community can become like-minded after a while. The search for like-mindedness is a response to our isolation and a longing for the predictability of Egypt. We might appreciate the wilderness as a vacation spot, or when we view it from the comfort of an overlook at the park. The fact is, we must travel into it to make the shift from contract to covenant, market to neighborliness.

FALLIBILITY

Neighborliness is based on the knowledge that fallibility is a permanent and natural condition. Fallibility is attentive to the limits of growth. It holds that the cost of development outweighs its attraction. It sees that death is not a problem to be solved, but a state that animates life. It appreciates that the planet is wounded and needs care for its restoration.

We can see clearly how accepting fallibility works by looking at the movement to include people who are called developmentally disabled. Their fallibility is far more visible than for most of us. If we approach them as though there is something we can do to fix them, rather than say their condition is a mystery, we do them a disservice.

> I was with someone in California a couple of weeks ago. He has a thirty-year-old son who, when he was four, got some kind of affliction and now, intellectually and emotionally, he's frozen at four. And the father says, "Thank God, it was four, and not two or thirteen." Then he says, "My son mediates to me God's grace every day."
>
> —John

When we acknowledge their mystery, we can move ahead with who they are. And that's what the disability movement is about. There's a parents' movement that got past the idea of finding a cure for their children. Instead, they say, this person has been a gift to me; this person has gifts and we're moving ahead. Their stance is that something understood as fallibility isn't something they're going to waste their lives pursuing. The belief in fallibility allows you the possibility of seeing what is there.

In contrast to the world of developmental disabilities, the reason there is so little community progress with people who are mentally ill is that they still live in the world of improvement. In other words, the idea is that we can cure them. With people who are developmentally disabled, it's pretty clear now that that's who they are, so there's much more communalization and effort with them than there are with people who are mentally ill.

The word *affliction* is often associated with fallibility. Its root is the Latin *afflictus,* distressed, the past participle of *affligere,* meaning to cast down. It is also a biblical word. There is the Bread of Affliction, which is the bread of Pharaoh, the bread the Israelites took with them into the wilderness. The apostle Paul says, "We are afflicted in every way, but not driven to despair."

These are some of the parallels between mystery and fallibility. We are perplexed by both of them but not destroyed; we are persecuted but not struck down. We can identify all the problems associated with them, but we haven't given in. We are comforted by the care of a trusted community.

Fallibility and mystery give rise to poetry, whereas the market depends on memos. And memos are prosaic unambiguous linear communication. This yields servitude. Fallibility yields freedom, with poetry and art as the methodology.

FAILING TO BE GOD

A forerunner of the modern corporation was created in the seventeenth century with the formation of the British East India Company which, backed up by the British military, opened the floodgates of colonialism. Its character negated all the neighborly qualities we are speaking of, both at home and abroad. The modern corporation began as a financing institution for projects such as railroads and tunnels that were too large for family or royal wealth to take on. Over time, it has taken on a larger meaning. It now aspires to be immortal. It aspires to perfection. It expects to live forever. With the corporation, the market asks us to sustain our immortality, to strive for perfection, to maintain dominance, to be in denial of our human condition.

So says the title John conceived for an essay he once wanted to write: "On the Incredible Possibilities of Failing to Be God." The cultural imperative of the market world is built on hubris, and it is in this way disabling. Its denial of the human condition is like something out of Greek myth; it is our Nemesis. The market culture has us aspire to be God, and the power that it has over us is called progress. It demands that we act as if we are not human. As if we are not in a finite place and in a limited universe. As if we are not going to die. William Paley was a founder of CBS and an iconic leader of the corporate market world. The author of his biography (Paper, 1987) reported Paley was the only person he knew whose last will and testament began, "If I die."

The practices of community, and neighborliness, with their common rituals of grief and celebration, are ways of dealing with the fact that we are not God.

GRIEF

Grief occurs to us because of the impossibility of perfection and immortality. The free market consumer ideology calls us to infinite possibility. It promises perfection (you can always improve your lot in life) and immortality (there is an answer to aging). This is its value proposition. Grow or die. Consume or be unhappy. The market is an engine for denial instead of grieving. In the market ideology, anything can be fixed. Denial is necessary to maintain the discipline of the market.

> My first wife slowly descended into alcoholism and died of it. And so we did everything we could along the way to try to cure her, fix her, stop her. All those things. And nothing worked. And it finally really depresses you. Nothing works.
>
> Ivan Illich came to visit and stayed with us. I was sitting with him one evening, telling him about everything that we had tried and how nothing had worked. "I just don't know what to do," I said. And he looked at me and said, "Then grieve."
>
> That had a really profound effect upon me. Beyond the world of fixing. Grief is the transforming experience.
>
> —John

Scripture can be read in the same way. Institutionalized misreading of the text says, "Let us skip over what does not affirm the market ideology. Let the market define what will recruit well and build the congregation." In *The Unbearable Lightness of Being*, Milan Kundera (1984) called that kind of religion "kitsch." Kitsch is religion that doesn't tell the truth about anything, most of all the ethics of the market.

One answer to the market call, then, is the action step of grief. Grief is an element of aliveness and the answer to the denial the market demands of us. It is an index of our humanity. It is proof of the presence of our relatedness to each other. It is a communal practice that recognizes that choosing the wilderness of vulnerability, mystery, and anxiety was a good and life-affirming choice.

THE COMMON GOOD

Abundance, mystery, fallibility, and grief create conditions to reclaim the common good. The commons cannot be fully reclaimed by a movement, or on a science- and fact-based or engineered, legislated, or problem-solving path alone. The efforts underway to restore the environment, to put land, air, water, and resources back into the hand of the public trust are essential. These efforts will only be complete, however, when there is shift in our way of being together and naming with our own voices—aliveness. It is our humanness that also needs restoration, and there is no way to reason our way there. This is why the language of covenant and fidelity must create an opening to transcend the dominant narrative of market and even the narratives of change management, development, and the world is your oyster.

3

ENOUGH IS ENOUGH

LIMITS OF THE MARKET IDEOLOGY

I am and there is no one besides me.

—Is. 47:8

Communities are realizing that something is missing in our capacity to raise a child, make a living, be healthy and safe. The shrinking middle class is just one of the consequences of the free market consumer ideology that draws us into this conversation. There are other signposts that we are near the end of a viable social infrastructure. The threat of planetary decline. Our fear for the well-being of the next generation.

One response is growing distrust and cynicism about the future. Cynicism always comes clothed in "realism." The alternative response is to begin with an act of imagination. Can we imagine another way? What do we need to do, individually and collectively, to imagine an alternative to the market, the system, the empire track? We might begin by seeing the consumer culture for what it is.

THE CONSUMER MARKET DISCIPLINES

The market's beliefs in scarcity, certainty, and perfection are embodied in a set of disciplines that keep it running smoothly and make it so seductive. Seeing them clearly gives us a choice.

The disciplines that we most need to question are surplus, control, speed, convenience, competition, and individualism. These are widely accepted ideas that promise, if we live by them, things will be best for all concerned. That Adam Smith's "invisible hand" will guide self-regulation and ultimately benefit the common good.

SURPLUS

The power of language is clear in the expression "free market." The market does many good things, but it does not set us free. The bars of market confinement are constructed of surplus. In the Old Testament wilderness, it was food that was not eaten in the day. Value it too much, save it for another day, and it spoiled. Now we call it profit. It is now compound interest. Surplus in the form of profit has become the sole criterion of value. It has become the point—even if nothing is produced in the process.

> I remember talking to an executive once about employee empowerment. I suggested something simple like unassigned spaces so that parking would be first come, first serve. That didn't seem to me to be too radical a step. And the executive said, "As soon as I give them a parking space they will have my salary."
>
> I was shocked, and then I thought he was right. We have come to identify ourselves by our assets, our surplus, our privilege.
>
> —Peter

We live in a time when a great deal of money comes from making money on money. Debt penalties. Derivatives, carrying capacities, and externalities. What was once called usury is now called good business. It's not just banks making money on money. GE at one point earned more money from financing aircraft engines than making them. Many businesses make more money on financing the customer purchase than on the product itself. That is why they give a discount if you open a credit card. Shipping and handling fees are a price increase if you buy online. Buy a computer, and then, at the register, you are urged to purchase a warranty. Guarantees that once came with a product now must be purchased separately as a clever form of price increase. Companies make money on rebates because, if they are complicated enough, 80 percent of customers won't file them. When it comes to our own money we are sold on the idea of interest, annuities, mutual funds, because you have to put your money to work. Financial advisors hate savings. You tell them you don't need any more money. They say you are a fool. No matter how much you have, it is not enough.

Andrew Carnegie sent out one of his people to find out how much money he had. The guy came back in two months and said, "I can't answer your question. There is no way. You have so much money there is no way you can capture and measure it all." And then Carnegie said he wanted to give most of it away. He couldn't do that either. He was vexed by compound interest. Warren Buffet has the same problem.

In Joshua Chapter 7, when Israel suffers a great military defeat, Joshua does an investigation and traces it down to the offending tribe and the offending guy. Joshua discovered that they lost because this guy Achan took something from the common good to add to his private collection. Achan says, "I saw the gold and silver and it was so shiny that I wanted it"; the narrative uses the word "covet" and refers to the Tenth Commandment. The desire for more called Achan to violate the common good for his own sake. That's today's argument for addiction: It was so shiny. It's also an argument for privatization.

The love of profit is central to the business perspective. The system keeps telling us that we have to have it. It explains why at the local

Rotary Club meeting, the first thing they do is report on the stock market results for the day. "Welcome. We need to get started. The market was up seven points today. Now let's get on with the meeting." The Dow Jones Industrial Average has become a sacrament of modern times. It comes before the meal, goes together with breaking bread. It is the prayer and benediction.

That's how love of surplus becomes a market liturgy. With sacraments like the DJIA, GNP/GDP, inflation rate, and economic growth rate, free market economics is raised to a spiritual practice. That discipline is what is under re-construction when we talk about the common good or a neighborly economy, especially if we talk of economic justice and equity and wealth redistribution, most commonly in the discussion of taxes and debt forgiveness.

The right use of wealth is an emotional and spiritual question. Most wealthy people are extremely generous, but the deeper generosity is willing to call into question who controls the capacities of production and wealth creation.

PREDICTABILITY AND CONTROL

The language of empire is one of the many ways the market exercises control in the consumer culture and avoids unexpected results. There's a place in Isaiah where the Assyrians threaten King Hezekiah and he tells them to speak Aramaic because if they speak Hebrew his people will understand and it will terrify them. Today the language of commerce is the universal tongue. The contract world wants business language to be the only acceptable way. The business perspective and globalization promote homogeneity and eliminate local culture.

John recalls hearing a story from Ivan Illich that dramatizes the culture's need for control and predictability and eventually made its way into *Shadow Work* (1981). As David Cayley (2015) tells it, Illich wrote an essay that begins with the story of Antonio Nebrija (1441–1522), a Spanish scholar who, in 1492, approached Queen Isabella of Spain in the hope of winning her support for his plan to write a formal grammar of the Castilian language. In that way he told her the untutored and unruly speech of her subjects could be brought under control and a new instrument of government could be created for the overseas dominions she was about to acquire—"language," he says, "has always been the consort of empire." Nebrija anticipated great things from Columbus's voyage to the West, then still in progress, but he tried to persuade the queen that his grammar might be an even more auspicious undertaking. Spain would acquire a language comparable to the languages of antiquity, and the wild speech of her peoples would be brought under domestic cultivation.

The Queen knew that the identity of a village or little town was very much tied to their language, and we know today it is still a critical part of culture. She told Nebrija how offensive it was in her mind to replace this local way of talking, a vernacular that keeps people together. It sustains their covenant.

When Nebrija comes back later, he argues that you can't have a nation and real power if you allow these local languages to endure. You've got to have a Mother Tongue. He finally won. King Ferdinand could see the point, and he and Isabella created the Mother Tongue. A centralized, consistent set of symbolic exchanges replaced the disciplines of unpredictable local cultures.

Illich always said the vernacular language was critical to a culture. Our tongue, our language, the vernacular is what the Mother Tongue assaulted. In recent times, the Basques were required to speak Castilian, the language of Madrid, not the Basque language. Madrid was trying to impose an imperial tongue, to stamp out local traditions.

In the corporate world you can hear a brand of Mother Tongue in the language of management. New ideas are rolled out. We make business cases. *Efficiency, bottom line, team players, can-do kind of people, cost is king, grow or die, downsizing, right-sizing, on-boarding, talent management, C-suite, take it to scale* are the Mother Tongue of systems. This is the language not of Queen Isabella, but the Business Perspective. A tool of commodification, of market empire. It stands in sharp contrast to the vernacular speaking the language of homemade, handmade, local made, language that is understandable to anyone, the language of neighbors and neighborhood.

Speed and Convenience

The free market consumer ideology is not just about money and surplus. It also has a romantic relationship with speed and convenience, the two core promises of technology. Technology and money are of the same nature: They make the case for the love of predictability, speed, and disruption. We think we control money, but it controls us. We think we control technology, but it defines us. It is a modern form of magic. So we accept the value of technology as self-evident. It represents unquestionable progress. But technology's place in our lives is a social construction, an artifact of the free market consumer ideology, not a given. And if it is a construction, then it can be constructed differently.

The Luddites understood that the machine was a challenge to a way of life and community. It was a fundamental change. It was the first manufacturing technology in human history that was independent of nature, geography, season, weather, sun, wind, human or animal power; it allowed humans for the first time to have an instant and unfailing source of production at their command.

The Luddite argument was that machinery destroyed community and the order of social relationships. The movement was against automation and, in an early form, globalization. The market's demand was to make something for another place and to specialize only in what are you are best at—just do that and purchase the rest. The machine-driven looms of Scotland created the consumer.

The idea that somehow you can live outside technological society is an illusion because its discipline is total. To be technologically illiterate is to place yourself outside the basic talk of everyday discourse. Techno-literacy becomes another Mother Tongue.

The Sale of Convenience

Convenience is the major selling proposition for technology. Our technology-supported lives have now become so convenient that we experience the practices of neighborliness as being greatly inconvenient. Walking. Handwriting. Borrowing sugar. Convenience is what the market sells. It is a surcharge added to the cost of community. The market's promised convenience and speed turn out to have a hidden cost.

The hidden cost of technology is an un-measured burden. What to do if my icemaker doesn't make ice or my automatic teakettle doesn't work? What if the computer goes down or is infected? In our romance with speed and convenience, the disruptions in our lives are masked. Plus, just because something is amazing, and useful and fast and cheap, doesn't mean it improves the quality of our lives or relationships with one another. Speed and convenience don't build neighborliness.

Technology has eradicated mystery and time. We need technology, but technology is not an adequate instrument for the maintenance of social life. When technology tries to operate as an end in itself, it magnifies its rightful place. To serve us well, technology has to be situated in some other explanatory narrative; in our case, it belongs as one small and useful piece of neighborliness and covenant.

CONVENIENCE DISPLACES CAPACITY

Convenience sells so well that we are no longer producers. At best we are hobbyists or do a little home repair. John's colleague Stan Hallet was raised on a farm in North Dakota. When Stan saw something that he liked, he would go home and make it. And he could fix anything. If something went wrong, he just enjoyed fixing it himself. All this came from the fact that he had lived in a world where he had to be a productive person on the farm. Which is why farmers traditionally specialize in collecting baling wire. You can fix anything with baling wire. It is the agrarian duct tape.

As we watch someone like Stan fix things around the house, we do not think what great skill he has; we think we could hire somebody to do that. What the free market consumer ideology has taken away from the neighborhood is the need and skill to be productive. This has been exchanged for all kinds of specialized activity, no matter what the system. There are specialists in medicine, transportation, child care, gardening, safety, even the Bible.

In most any group of people, if you go around the room and ask, "What can you do?" no one talks about being able to make something.

They give mostly service and relational answers. I can love people. I can pray. I have professional skills. We have been deskilled in what it takes to produce community. Our incapacity is like being disembodied. It makes us useless. This incapacity is epitomized in our teenagers. The teen years are that period in people's lives when they are told that they are useless, except for performing in school. We think the job of teenagers is to go to school and get good grades. And if they don't, they have failed at an early age. No kindness in this.

Neighborliness calls for reclaiming neighborhood community skill across whole array of possibilities. This is what E.F. Schumacher was talking about when he wrote *Small Is Beautiful* (1975). The Schumacher Institute was at the beginning asking what were tools that people could make locally and use locally that will solve all kinds of problems that we are paying big systems to fix. The focus was on tools for local production. This made the case for appropriate technology, the tools that build us.

The Amish are another example. The Amish test any invention against its impact upon their community. There's a famous story about the guy who was surprised to see an Amish farmer using a motorized threshing machine. He stopped to ask the farmer about it and said, "I thought that the Amish didn't believe in machines. That you never would go in a car, that you wouldn't thresh your wheat with this machine with a motor in it." And the farmer said, "We test all the machines. This threshing machine helps us be productive here, but the car separates us." It's a great insight. The Amish are looking at technology consciously. In deciding whether to allow technology, the test is: What does it do to our covenant?

DIGITAL SOLUTIONS

Technology is always expanding its ownership of the community space. Nextdoor.com is an Internet product to connect neighbors. It is constructed to be a vehicle for connection and generosity. When people need something—paint, someone to clean house, a way to recycle an unneeded mattress—they post it and find a supplier or a taker. Twenty-five percent of nextdoor.com is a home-based flea market. Another twenty percent promises safety. You use it to tell your neighbors about crime in the area.

In one sense this technology is an invitation to become engaged. Every day in any neighborhood you get thirty or so nextdoor.com messages. Every day they welcome five new members. Nextdoor.com is simulating the welcoming of community. Its limitation is that currently it isn't collectivizing groups in the neighborhood. They are working on this; the face-to-face relationship is the next step they are after. The question is: How do you move to that?

We work with a couple of very creative college students who are trying to do something with that precise intention: to use the Internet to get people face-to-face in service or creating something. They tried it rather intensively in several communities, and by and large it didn't work. The technology works to bring people together socially, commercially, and to invest, but has not yet built the productive capacity of a neighborhood.

THE MEANING OF MONEY

When he heard this, he was sad; for he was very rich.

—Luke 18:23

We are living in an economy that speaks of freedom, but believes in control, surplus, and growth. These ideas are sustaining the empire. They explain the way we think about money and how it defines and controls us. The work is to face the question of how money may serve us, rather than how we serve money.

The dominance of the market empire is endless. Thousands of U.S. high school students play stock market simulation games every year. At a private school in Texas, the Board of Trustees raised $100,000 so the kids can play the stock market with real money (Yousuf, 2013). It doesn't get any clearer than that: The stock market is the modern tabernacle.

Or consider the Junior Achievement program. It has been introduced as a legitimate extracurricular activity into school systems across the country. Its purpose is to teach students in kindergarten through the twelfth grade to value the free market and experience the joys of acquisition. It says, in effect, this is the task of school: to teach you how to start a business, to manage a portfolio, to think entrepreneurially.

Exploring the meaning of money includes asking: What does poverty mean? Poverty is not simply the absence of money. It is the absence of possibility and the effect of living outside the consumer economy. If you give money to poor people, it helps, but is not decisive in lifting them out of the mindset and exclusion that poverty represents. That is why charity and programs within the market ideology have limits.

The poor and the rich are both out of relationship with money and our construction of it. When we speak of an economy of generosity or a core economy or an underground economy or a non-monetized economy, it sounds utopian to the ears of the market world. The point about money is that we have to disconnect it from any notion we have about the quality of life. Money has nothing to do with the quality of life. It needs to be brought back into its original use, which is to be just a medium of exchange.

So what's the right relationship with money? Money is not a point and not a purpose. It was an invention to ease trade, and now it has become the primary measure of our value, of how we talk about each other; it defines how productive our lives have been.

MONEY AND THE MACHINE

Enclosure got people off the land, and the advent of the machine in the late 1700s accelerated their movement to the city. Mechanization required cheap labor and production control. Factories needed workers, and managers. In *The Meaning of the City*, sociologist Jacques Ellul (1970) offers the idea that the city was created because of Cain's losing covenant with God and being punished by being allowed to live. Cain expected God to strike him dead because he had killed his brother, but God said, "No. I will mark you, but you are going to live." Cain didn't know how to cope with being alive and out of covenant with God. This created the need to huddle with others in order to manage their alienation from God, so Cain organized the first city, Nimrah.

Urbanization and the loss of community can be thought of as partly economic, partly a path to sustain empire, and partly the result of losing our connection with God and each other. In Scotland, if you were exiled, thrown out, or somehow detached from your clan, you would be called a "broken person." Broken people are people without community, which is really a death sentence. In today's terms, they are the casualties of empire and industrialization.

This is not an argument against urban life, in any sense. The city does bring us closer to each other. We do need to see clearly, though, that the large worldwide migration to the city, while driven by a desire for a better life, has the side-effect of separating people from their own culture, habits, memories, and ritual ways of living a life. Part of the promise of restoring neighborhoods is to create local culture, with memory and affection, to replace what was left behind.

WISHING FOR SAFETY, BELIEVING IN GROWTH

Everybody with some sense knows that what they are doing isn't satisfying. For the last thirty years everybody in a leadership position, in every institution, has called for change. A common practice to initiate reform is to see what other systems are doing: It's called benchmarking. You copy what others do and call it innovation. The market and system language for this whole process is *change management*. The benchmark is based on imitation; it is someone else's standard. It gives hope where people are seeking methodology, but it is this way of seeking methodology that keeps anything fundamental from changing.

Practices like benchmarking do put the agenda of change on the table though. Unfortunately, no matter how serious we are, we immediately discover that the change is costly, risky, and not what we had in mind. In the Hebrew Bible, as soon as the Israelites took two steps into the wilderness, they were in freefall. They wanted to go back. They remembered the steady food supply. We don't want to depart that far from our Egypt. "Egypt" is predictable. Secure. We hold the belief that predictability and control make us safe.

However, we are now at the place where the experience of more and more people is that the institutional empire's protection is disappearing. The so-called well-being and safety that the system provides are now reaching their limits. We see limits to the planet, to jobs, to our health, to our children. They come in the language of student debt, income inequality, lower than expected health measures, pockets of deep unemployment, concern for the environment, balance of payments, stalemated politicians, and wars without end. It's clear that the idea— supported by all of our elected officials, business and activist leaders, and the media—is to try to get back on the market and system track. The answer is growth. Growth, growth, and more growth.

In other words, we think that the force that took us to the limit is the solution. That what we need is more of a consumption-driven economy. Every public narrative is on that track, the track that led to the cliff. The free market consumer ideology has so captured our discourse that anybody who speaks of any other approach sounds like a nut. Especially in elected office.

Finding the right politicians, regardless of their beliefs, will make a difference, but only in limited ways. We will find the right politicians as soon as we have reclaimed our own place in the wilderness. No need to worry about the politicians at this moment, because they are a product of our consciousness. We are creating them.

COMPETITION AND CLASS

Do not be hard-hearted or tight-fisted toward your needy neighbor.
—Deut. 15:7

The market rests on a religious belief in competition, which means that for you to win, I must lose. This idea is so deeply embedded in the culture that competition is held to be part of the nature of being human, despite the anxiety it creates. Now I am not in friendship with my neighbor; I am in competition with my neighbor. Their name is Jones.

I only found one book, in my years of university teaching, that really challenged deeply the thinking of students. It's called *No Contest: The Case Against Competition,* written by Alfie Kohn (1992). That became the only book that I always assigned to students.

The reason it was such a challenge is that those kids in my classes lived, and had thrived, in a culture of competition. It is so pervasive that this book was the first time they had ever had anybody, in at least words or thought, putting forward all kinds of evidence that they had a bad assumption. The book presents evidence, both in stories and a lot of research, showing how cooperative activities beat competition at whatever game we play or result we seek.

—John

In the first year of school we start grading on the curve. This means that you have to have classmates who will take a D so that you can get a B, because in school there are not enough A's or B's for all of us to have them. Success is scarce. In worshipping the bell-shaped curve, we put Napoleonic hats on the heads of first-graders, seven-year-olds, and we tell them, "Up to now, you have learned for the pure pleasure of learning. Now you must compete with other learners. Find others in the class who will take the hit for you or you must take the hit for them."

Not too long ago, in school, at the end of every week there was a spelling test and it was graded by the teacher over the weekend. On Monday morning she reassigned the seats in the classroom so the person who had the highest score sat right up in front, next to the window or door. The kid with the next-highest score was assigned the next seat up front, and so on, right through the room. If you sat in the back right-hand corner you were the dumbest kid in the room. And everybody knew it. Every week the results of the competition were reconfirmed. That's not education, that's tyranny.

After you've built a wagon with square wheels over and over again, a round wheel is not too hard to invent. For our culture, that wheel is called cooperation. What we're trying to remind ourselves about the culture of competition is what a round-wheeled wagon looks like. You first have to understand that you're in a culture that commands you without your ever knowing you're commanded.

Class by Design

One assumption in the free market narrative is that an underclass is inevitable. That it is in the nature of low-labor-cost capitalism and competition. What is the cost of an underclass? Who is to say there should be no underclass?

Theologically, the underclass is against God's will. It also makes society unworkable for the vast majority. One manifestation of that un-workablility is violence. The prophets, particularly Amos and Jeremiah, talk about the violence that is perpetrated against the vulnerable. It's a class war conducted from above. Class war is always conducted from above, but it's the people from above who immediately cry war if you point out any social differentiations.

This claiming from above that economic justice is class warfare trumps friendship and reason. After we spoke about these issues once in Milwaukee, a good friend, a successful executive, an active and compassionate leader in his company and in the city, said at the end, "You are talking class warfare." Maybe he was right. It appears that the wealthy characteristically want social differentiations to remain hidden, because if we make them visible, then something has to happen.

The argument goes like this: Lifting up the underclass is costly. The cost is that if they get a piece of the pie, then I get a smaller piece. Even if I have more pie than I can eat, I might get hungry in the middle of the night. But you never have enough in a competitive system. You will never have enough until you have the whole pie. And a pie to spare. Regardless of how full you are or how much you have.

Class Warfare and the Distribution of Wealth

It is the triad of widows and orphans and immigrants who are the most vulnerable in a patriarchal, market-dominated society. If you are an orphan or a widow, you don't have a man, with special rights, to defend you, and obviously immigrants don't have any rights or protector either. So the argument of the Torah, particularly the Book of Deuteronomy, shows up in the Prophets: The community has an obligation to protect these three vulnerable types because they don't have any other protection.

Alongside the issue of how to treat widows, orphans, and immigrants is the question of prisoners. The United States has the greatest mass incarceration of prisoners in the world. We also have the most private enterprises owning correctional institutions. The three texts related to this are Isaiah 61, Psalm 146, and Matthew 25. All are about reaching out to prisoners.

If we believe that economic provision must be made for these vulnerable people, the economy must be subordinated to the viability of society. The Torah is concerned that these people should not become a permanent underclass economically. And therefore you have the Law of Release, the provisions for welfare, and the Jubilee Year to keep them as viable participants in the economy.

It's a Commandment in Deuteronomy 15 that says every seven years people have to be released from debt. The first verse just says people have to be released, but the rest of the law says that poor people have to be released from debt. This is a text that says you will always have the poor with you.

The class warfare discussion—the discussion of "Why don't the poor work harder?"—is a mild collision between our free market narrative and the Torah. The consumer culture has marginalized the widows, orphans, and immigrants. What stands out is every time you teach about the cancellation of debts for poor people, someone raises a hand and says, "There is no evidence that they really ever did that." That's the only text in the Bible that holds an imperial danger: the text that speaks about subordinating the economy to the common good.

A church friend and I never have lunch that he doesn't rail against food stamps. He is so worried that somebody is going to get something for nothing.

Is he worried about going hungry? No.

Then why is he worried about somebody getting something for nothing? What's behind that? Because everybody ought to work. That's his slogan. Everybody ought to work for what they get. He believes in the autonomous person.

What he misses is that poor people work harder than rich people. That's not known. What interests me, of course, is that he never raises any questions about what unearned gifts he might have received. And it only recently occurred to me that he never raises any questions about the huge subsidies to business and industry, which are all something for nothing. But speak of those food stamps or those "poor people," and it touches a deep emotional chord.

—Walter

The Myth of Individualism

What sustains the class system, the empire, and the free market narrative is the myth of individual development. We cling to the hope that it serves the common good. It doesn't. It does serve the individual. Beautifully.

Based on our faith in the individual, we have trained hundreds of thousands of people inside companies in an effort to democratize the culture and build relatedness at work. It has had little effect. It made all of their marriages better and the smartest ones left: Thank you, I'm awake, I'm alive, good-bye. AT&T trained 5,000 people on humanizing their interactions. At the end of the training, if you asked them, "Has this culture shifted at all?" they would say, "No, it hasn't been touched, but we loved the training."

What is needed now is to focus on collective transformation. A communal transformation. You see signs of it emerging. In the business world we have social entrepreneurs and conscious capitalism. It is a positive step. It does not, however, question the totalizing narrative. If you look inside those movements, you realize they still deeply believe in a consumer and free market economy.

The social entrepreneurs and conscious capitalists are trying to be kinder to their employees and better serve their customers and suppliers. The next step is to imagine that the common good calls for more than that: It calls us to question surplus. Question globalization. Commit to local livelihood, food that rots, neighborhoods that raise children. To imagine that the purpose of an enterprise can be communal.

A scarcity and monopoly economy creates a context in which considering alternatives—an economy of generosity or core economy or an underground economy or a non-monetized economy—makes no sense. The context just does not give those options relevance. This is the power of the market ideology in which we swim.

4

TENTACLES OF EMPIRE

You gave me no water for my feet . . .you gave me no kiss . . .you did not anoint my head with oil.

—Luke 7:44–46

In Cuernavaca in the 1960s Ivan Illich had a discussion about institutional evolution with people from around the world. He was very prophetic in saying that you could trace the community benefits of institutions through time. They rise and then flatten out and then they begin to recede and move in the opposite direction for which the institution was created. He called that counter-productivity. In fact, he said, this process was what we were observing at the moment, so that in the end you would have crime-making justice systems. You would have sickness-making medical systems. You would have stupid-making schools. All are a manifestation of how the tentacles of empire reach into every corner of our lives.

THE CORPORATIZATION OF SCHOOLS

Our schools are one place where the strength of the empire is especially clear.

Universities are increasingly marketplace-driven. They are revising their curricula away from the humanities and promoting programs dictated by industry that off-load the cost of education onto the public. They are growing their educational customer base by giving students more flexibility as a recruiting device. University of Kansas used to have seventy-two required courses to graduate. Now they have fifty hours of core curriculum, all designed to be more adaptive to the changing marketplace. They don't want people to have to take courses that aren't immediately useful to them. The humanities now have to justify their contribution to the economy, instead of to the quality of citizenship of the student. All this is the market ideology running higher education for the executive class and workplace training for the employees.

Also, our schools have moved to the frontline of the class warfare being waged. The argument is that in a global market our elite have to be able to compete with Japan and China and Brazil for the best and brightest. For all others, we need cheap labor. This is a disinvestment strategy toward urban and rural un-privileged families and youth. It holds the belief that a small minority of well-educated people can sustain an economy that pays low wages for everybody else. It says that all people do not need to be well educated.

NO VIEW FROM THE TOP

The people who are in charge of the corporations, the market system's institutions, have an interest in staying blind to social and economic deprivation and differentiation. They may know about it and buy tables at fundraisers, but they do not see it. They don't see it because they think they are contributors and cause to the well-being of society. They would say they have, through mass production, brought benefits to people who never had them before. They have a foundation through which they give money back to communities. They transform their companies into green ones. Their buildings are LEED-certified buildings.

The challenge is that these benefits never reach the bottom of the system. The rising tide does not lift all boats. Those at the bottom and at the margin are considered undeserving; they are today's equivalent of scripture's widows, orphans, and immigrants. They are considered undeserving because from a distance they seem "unproductive." This is what the free market consumer ideology system can't tolerate. We blame them for not producing. We say they don't contribute. There is no awareness of how hard it is to have little. This is the unforgiveable sin of the market ideology.

The market ideology declares that to be a widow, orphan, or immigrant— or to be unemployed—is a self-inflicted wound. It's your fault. We associate undeserving with the people on the margins. What is changing is that the middle class is slowly joining the widows, orphans, and immigrants.

Charity is the instrument or means to sustain that mentality. Charity does not address the economy. It takes the economy as a given and attends to its casualties. Most of the churches are so proud of their charity that you can't even talk about the economy. After we made a presentation on this line of thinking in one of our churches, someone said, "I saw that and I prayed for you because it looked like you were stepping over the line."

END OF ALIVENESS

One way to think of the market ideology and the empire is that it produces alienation and loss of human vitality. When you have stolen someone's humanity it leaves the person pointless and with a deep sense of entitlement. You have taken aliveness out of life. The system isolation is not only omnipresent but it is aggressive and compelling, attractive, and seductive. It operates as if the dominant culture is all there is. This is a socio-economic and political reality. An alternative path requires a prophecy, an idea, and a plan that has the capacity to resist the compelling force of the culture of isolation in which we find ourselves.

The consumer culture's belief in invincibility and progress makes for a culture that is afraid of death. This fear fuels a system that offers accumulation, speed, and convenience as a defense against death. The culture flows from the assumption that the accumulation of commodities will make us safe and happy. This thinking touches everything about politics, economics, and distorted religion. There is a tacit collusion among all of these forces that causes our human capacity to shrivel. We abandon our sense of being human together. What makes it so difficult is that you can't just address this issue or that issue because they are all interrelated.

Within this framework, there is no alternative future. The most the market can imagine is grander extensions of the present. No interruption, no miracle, no surprise, no gift. No prophecy. There is, of course, disruption and innovation in every industry, but it all occurs within the market ideology. New technology is disruptive by design, but never questions technology itself. The technology world loves to disrupt markets by increasing speed and convenience. The financial rewards are magical. So now you can order a ride from Uber, but they'd never try to disrupt the market system. The Uber-ride is contained inside that box.

A consumer culture that takes the aliveness out of life also rewards senselessness; there is something senseless about this modern world. In death you can't use your senses. You say people are brain dead because their senses are useless. What we have in our technology and the culture that surrounds us are systematic ways of limiting our senses. It's non-sense we're dealing with. The alternative is to be sensible. In his book on why Jews keep kosher on Sabbath and don't work on Saturday, Michael Fishbane (2008) says they do it to stay mindful. And mindfulness, he says, is essential in a mindless or senseless society.

MOBILITY AND ISOLATION

When standard of living becomes the measure of well-being, mobility becomes the norm. It takes precedence over family and place. It carries a cost. We have seen it in the larger culture where the job moved us around at will. We see it in young people living very fluid lives.

Peter was in a small group one night with a sincere young man who made two statements. The first was that he had grown up alone and had a lot of time to himself. He was enormously lonely. He is about thirty, and his desire is to find connection with the world, to be more related to others.

The second statement was in response to the question "What would it take to get you out of the house and into the neighborhood?" He said, "Nothing." He said he moves every year. He lives with a bunch of guys, and every year, when a couple of them take off and get married or move out of town, they reconstitute their living arrangements. "I move every year so I don't care about my neighborhood," he said. "There is nothing you can do to make me care about where I live."

Mobility and isolation work hand in hand in the empire narrative. One manifestation is that when people value mobility they are isolated. Spiritual life and relational life become disassociated from place. To move geographically or up a system ladder separates us from those left behind. To keep moving from one place to another means people have no story in place and no story in work. That makes an isolated population, without a story of connection and aliveness. We come to think that isolation is the norm, and this leaves people ripe for manipulation and seduction. You don't have a story, but you can buy a new refrigerator. And it is amazing that a refrigerator can be more seductive than a people with a story. Commodity replaces narrative.

In the neighborhood, the people on the margins are the most unsafe. The rest of us have moated ourselves in the suburbs. We have automatic garage doors. Backyards. No front porches. This separates us from the people on the margin. We also warehouse the elderly, who suffer from great loneliness. When Peter takes his granddaughter to a piano lesson in a Senior Center, everything stops when Gracie walks into the room. Not because of who Gracie is, but because they are hungry to be in a broader community so they can experience all the gifts of other friends and neighbors.

UN-PRODUCTIVE WEALTH

Wealth now comes from trading currencies, derivatives, futures, and other forms of making money on money. It is trading that produces nothing of value from three hundred trillion dollars exchanged every day. This is modern, legitimized usury—far away from the face-to-face personal relationship between the producer and the consumer that is essential to put us into a more authentic relationship with money.

When we buy from a corporate or big box entity, we take money out of local circulation. This turns neighbors into adversaries. The Tenth Commandment is about coveting your neighbor's things: I want more money, a bigger house, and more stuff. The market narrative calls me to want everybody's money, and your wanting money constitutes a threat to me.

The biblical understanding is you cannot accept interest payments from members of the community. You can charge interest to outsiders, but not your neighbors. The thinking is that community is face-to-face, neighborly covenanting. Usury will distort that. You don't have a covenant with strangers, so there is no special bond to distort. The biblical world understood the destructive nature of interest or surplus, not just in the way it put an end to neighborly relations but also how it constructed a distant and instrumental relationship with the stranger.

In a world where the neighborhood is obsolete, the making of money on money becomes legitimate. From whom and what it is based on is irrelevant. That is the way money becomes not a means of transaction, but an economy itself.

VIOLENCE

The current discourse about violence is another expression of the tentacles of empire and the scarcity and class distinctions of the market culture. The conversation on violence becomes one about gun control and retribution. When we talk about gun control, it's always formulated as someone else's issue. In most safety and violence conversations, we are never talking about our own violence. Nor would it occur to the nightly news that the news itself was participating in creating what it reported on.

It may be that the gun violence is the end point of a process by which the adults became isolated from the young people in their communities. As the whole adult world separated from its village-task of raising children, the children made their own village. And we named them gangs. People who are in a gang call it "my family." They are young people who have tried in some way to create their own family, because the family that they come from isn't able to raise them in a competitive world and the village has lost its capacity to raise them, too. And that process has been going on for a better part of a century. Guns in hand have been added to the equation, but guns didn't cause any of this. Guns are just a new tool introduced to children creating family among peers.

Lord of the Flies was the ultimate expression of the absence of parenting, exposing the violent effects of the lack or mistrust of authority (Golding, 1959). This particular issue of violence has to do with the failure of the villages to raise a child. And the alternative is not to focus on violence; the focus is how to create in our neighborhood the villages that can raise children.

ILLUSION OF REFORM

Talk of reform is always on the table. The call for reform is most often about trying harder at what is not working. Reform in the context of empire, in the context of scarcity, is all about better management and more automated processes. Health care reform is about reducing costs and increasing efficiency. School reform is about more certification and releasing bad teachers. Government reform is about lowering costs and taxes.

In the face of opposition, or evidence that the human or environmental costs are too high, empire adopts these kinds of reform as a guise to pretend it is healing itself. This is called reform, but it is really cosmetic change, which promotes more of what it is. Totalitarian regimes always have to call things by a name of false promise. The corporate commitment to immortality is called "succession planning." Failures are called "development opportunities." Innocent civilian victims are called "collateral damage." Eliminating a thousand jobs is called "right-sizing." Eliminating a million jobs is called "restructuring the job market." Development is the watchword of empire, giving a positive face to its penchant for colonization. "Development" means that if you are not doing well there is something wrong with you. If you are a country, then there are financial austerities that you have to follow. If you are an individual, then we make coaching and mentoring available to you.

What transforms is something other than what we call reform, or privatization, or development. Transformation is a shift in beliefs and an alternative narrative that follows those beliefs. It is an act of imagination that is open to the wilderness of the Exodus narrative. It is applying the language of covenant and neighborliness to the challenges of raising children, healing the earth, becoming healthy, and creating an economy that works for all. It begins with a shift in language and narrative. It continues by re-authorizing whose voices are listened to. It completes the effort with action that is small, slow, and produced by people nearby. It requires language and action that seeks a future outside the system world of solutions.

5

THE COMMON GOOD IS THE NEW FRONTIER

My house shall be called a house of prayer for all peoples.

—Is. 56:7

As part of enclosure, the Scots were driven off the land and replaced with sheep. The peasant farmers weren't producing enough income, and you could make more money raising sheep. Most of the Scots who emigrated left because they were forced off their land. By forcing people off the land, the private landowners created a desert and called it freedom. And that was the end, in essence, of the commons in Scotland.

What was disabled was a set of practices embedded in that culture. Free market ideas replaced the practices that had made up the Scots' culture. To depart the consumer culture, the viewpoint of the commons is a way to create, in our own place, a homeland and to reclaim a culture that, in fact, was never forgotten. We are looking for the context for a culture of neighborliness. The commons is what some would call that context—the elements that would allow neighborliness to happen, the nest from which the neighborly culture can grow.

THE NEIGHBORLY COVENANT

Covenant is central to the experience of community and the commons. Covenants are not required in the market world, which places its trust in contracts. Agreements have to be stated, in contracts. A covenant is built on vows in which more is implied than stated. Think again of a wedding vow, in which much is implied and you don't know what form the future is going to take.

Using the language of community and covenant opens up possibilities. For example, covenant language uses vows and neighborly agreements to speak of money and our relationship to it, and to one another. It brings freedom and relatedness into the conversation. It's not bargaining, it's not bartering, and it's not an exchange. It is an invitation to covenantal justice, a call to create a more just or equitable world based on covenant. It's a vow that we take to each other. It's a commitment we make to our neighbors all around us for its own sake.

In many ancient cultures, merchants and traders were financed by people outside the community. It was the unwelcome outsider who made the local economy function. In modern times the outsiders still control the local economy. It is people outside the neighborhood who own the major means of production and consumption. The neighbor's role is to watch the money leave town.

The ancient Jews would from time to time forsake community for market reasons. In a text in Nehemiah the rich Jews are taxing the poor Jews and the poor Jews are having to mortgage their farms in order to pay interest on their debt. What needs to be said about the rich Jews taxing poor Jews is that they were doing that to collect taxes for the Persian Empire; they had signed on for the Empire against their own people. Nehemiah scolds them and forces them to enter into a covenant with one another because they were violating the Torah of doing that against members of the community.

Religion has from the beginning held this as its purpose: to find the "way" away from the "track." In Judaism Torah is called The Way. In the New Testament, Christians were called "followers of the way" before they were called Christians. The concept of the Tao signifies a way, path, or route. So the path is always an alternative to the track laid down by the dominant value system.

Our social situation constantly tries to adjudicate between the track of the consumer market, which has such a compelling power and such visible payouts, and a path, which we are naming neighborliness, that lacks those visible rewards but is in sync with who we really want to be. We move back and forth and try to reconcile that tension all the time.

The market track might be thought of as mechanistic and guided by reason. The neighborly path is associated with personal gifts and is guided by the spirit. On the path, we are not guided by equations and algorithms. We are guided by covenant; it is only through that sacred agreement that we gain access to mystery and fallibility, which define our humanness.

The wish for safety in the free market consumer culture makes certainty enormously attractive. In the neighborly culture, certainty gives way to mystery, fallibility, and covenant. Our work is to sustain a covenant with each other and with the common good.

It is not unlike the work arising from the question "What could the modern church do to reconstitute itself?" The rise of globalization, the intensification of the expansion of the market, has put us out of covenant with our neighbors and with God. And we've lost our covenantal language, which means we've lost our memory. And so how can we think about the re-covenanting process of localizing our culture and economy?

The church has to have a conversation about what the communal disciplines that affirm faith are. It begins with a consciousness of the taken-for-granted disciplines of the market to which we all blindly adhere. This is the beginning way for the market disciplines to lose their power: examining the resistances to covenant. "You do not have enough, therefore you are not enough" is a powerful belief sustaining the market. The faith communities must believe "You are enough, and therefore you have enough."

And so must we all.

THE COMMONS

America was not founded on a belief in the common good. The people who came to settle in the Massachusetts Bay Colony were like-minded, but the source of their well-being was not the commons; it was the divine right of kings and their representatives, now in the form of the Massachusetts governor. Kings were commissioned by God, and it was God who therefore gave John Winthrop the right to govern. When people like Roger Williams declared that the right to rule came from the people, he was sentenced to death. He narrowly escaped the soldiers sent after him and went on to found Rhode Island. The price for publicly arguing for the commons was exile.

In his book *Lincoln at Gettysburg: Words That Remade America*, Garry Wills (2006) argues that it was Lincoln in the Gettysburg Address who transformed America's individualism-oriented Constitution, with all its checks and balances, into a vision of the common good. Lincoln is the de facto godfather of the common good.

Almost any notion of the common good butts up against the ideology of individualism. One contrast between the United States and more communal cultures such as Sweden is that our individualism runs so deep that it is practically the American creed—as if you can't get from there to the common good. Our commitment to the individual blocks out the neighbor and the neighborhood because all I care about is myself. It seeks a world of like-minded individuals. It dismisses communal-minded cultures like Sweden's as socialist.

The commons is the modern stance for a life not centered on profit and wealth. Belief in the commons says there are resources and wealth that belong to us all. It is reversing enclosure. It is a secular, political break with the commercial empire. The commons is a stance against empire that calls for the circular flow of money, for wealth to be returned to local hands. For example, in hard times, it calls for money to be created by the government instead of by interest-bearing loans from the private sector. Radical? Perhaps, but the Bank of North Dakota has been doing this since 1919.

The whole co-operative movement is another example of an alternative to the dominant market economy. It reconstructs purpose. It says that the purpose of the business is to build community and to care for the commons. It is the alternative to privatization and empire.

The first book that sociologist Robert D. Putnam (1993) wrote was a study of the economic differences between northern and southern Italy, northern Italy being very modern and productive and southern Italy not. This investigation led him to focus on associations. He found that southern Italy had very little associational activity, whereas northern Italy did and that the nature of the business development in the north had grown out of "associational forms," that is, sets of relationships among people. Putnam's idea was that money and the development of business is a relational activity.

In other words, local businesses are a mirror image of local associational life. That life is just taking place with a different mode of communication, which we call money. This view is a step in the search for an alternative to the globalization mindset. It restores community and our humanity.

AN ALTERNATIVE SOCIAL ORDER

Neighborliness is what was found in the Old Testament wilderness. It boils down to a care for the commons, care for the well-being of the whole, that which we hold for the sake of all. Neighborliness welcomes all into community. It stands for hospitality, the welcoming of the stranger.

The market ideology produces outsiders as a side-effect; they are another externalized cost of doing business. If you are well off it serves you well to be unwilling to acknowledge the poor. To acknowledge the underclass as gifted human beings, instead of labeled people, is destabilizing to empire. The market ideology needs explanations for the poor and the marginalized that keep the load on them. We claim it is their psychology, their culture, their education, the breakdown of the family. All of these rationalizations avoid questioning the market system. They become an implicit collective agreement to create a class structure. These responses are not about the money, for the well-off could lift up the underclass at no cost to themselves. They sustain the breakdown of the commons, the evaporation of culture, driven by the market mentality.

When the commons evaporates, so does the culture. A culture is a group of people, in a place, that has a story, a history; it has a particular language, and a narrative, but it doesn't have laws and rules in the formal sense. It tells you what "our way" is, but it isn't written in a book. It's not explicit. It's in the language of the people. David Cayley (2015) again reminds us that Ivan Illich sought a name for that portion of social life that had been, remained, or might become immune to the logic of economization. His candidate was "vernacular."

If you go to a neighborhood and the people there say, "Well, the way we have handled X is . . . ," then you know that neighborhood is a transforming place because it has a memory. In most modern neighborhoods you never hear anybody say that. Nobody would say, "Well, our way here on Judson Avenue is. . . ." A culture consists of habits, and Robert Bellah and his colleagues (1985) talk about "habits of the heart." You do things in a particular way, and the young are socialized into it: "This is how we do it." In a consumer market system, the young are socialized into performance, entertainment, and acquisition. Not local place, local story, and communal memory.

The loss of our memory of the commons carries with it the loss of un-commodified friendship. Angeles Arrien (1993) claimed that in all of us, across all traditions and cultures, there is buried within an experience of collective life, even if it has faded. No matter our upbringing, there is a collective memory of neighborly life on our streets, in our churches, in our local businesses. It was what once powered society. Now if you use the word *collective* too often, you are associated with socialism and communism. This is the kickback from a market ideology fueled by autonomy and the triumph of the individual. This kickback does not just come from a politicized media, or the private sector; it also comes from our family members and even friends.

RESISTING THE EMPIRE

In Wales, speaking Welsh is still a live issue against the conforming and controlling effects of empire and the Mother Tongue. It's an aftershock of the time when England developed numerous ways to break the Gaelic language. The English saw stamping out Gaelic as essential to finally putting Scotland under control, so they made the punishment for speaking the language death by hanging. The organizing question was: How do you break the culture of locality? The English answer was very instructive. They outlawed the bagpipe, they outlawed the kilt, and they outlawed the language.

Many Presbyterian churches now have one day every year when everyone in the community puts a kilt on and marches into church with bagpipes. It's a claim to their Scottish roots, but what happens is that all kinds of people who never come to church get out their kilts and come to church once a year. It may be chauvinistic, but it's an act of independence, a relic of the Scots' resistance to the English. Mardi Gras is a similar example, as are customs like celebrating the Feast of San Gennaro or the Día de los Muertos. All are acts of defiance against the mother culture, ways of keeping a local, minority, and neighborhood culture alive and well.

Observance of the Sabbath is also a protest against the restless productivity of the commercial culture. Think of the battle over Sunday closing laws. The blue laws. For a long time, in many places, you couldn't have businesses open on Sunday. This was evidence of the church's awareness of the destructive power of commerce. Often this struggle against the market empire was conducted in very legalistic ways, but it was a campaign fought on many levels.

Once upon a time Pennsylvania had a law that no inning of baseball for the Phillies or the Pirates could begin after 6 p.m. on Sunday because on Sunday night you went to church. In St. Louis and other longstanding baseball cities, clergy can still go to baseball games for a dollar. The reason is that when the teams started Sunday baseball they were afraid of resistance from the church. So clergy were given cheap tickets, but they had to sit in the upper seats.

The battle is over now. Sunday is open for business.

OFF-MARKET POSSIBILITIES

Off-modern is a term used in discussing art. There is modernism, there is post-modernism, and where do you go after that? Post-post. This has led to the term off-modern, which means we have to think of art in a context that sets modernism and its stage of development aside.

The possibility we call neighborliness might be called off-market; it represents a future where the market no longer is the center of our conversation and the market's requirements no longer shape us like a Procrustean bed. So speed, convenience, cost, efficiency, the business perspective, and the rest become no longer central to culture. They thrive, they matter, but they exist on the margin of our consciousness.

In the Bible both the Moses movement and the Jesus movement were radically off-market. They both called people to radical disciplines that resisted the powers that be. In the Moses movement you get the Ten Commandments, which are anti-Pharaoh mandates, and in the Jesus movement you get the Beatitudes, which are an imagination against Rome, the Roman Empire. The alternative to the market of the consumer culture is another kind of market, a local-producer place of exchange. An example is your community farmers market. This market keeps money local, moving in a circular way to serve the common good. Quite different from Wall Street, where the only point is to make money on money.

> I used to go fairly frequently to Cuernavaca, a small city outside of Mexico City. Twice a week they had a market in a huge building. Everything in the market was from an individual producer or an individual distributer. It was rich, almost prolific. Locally produced and mass-market commodities were both there, but the spirit and the meaning of that market in that community was about the community, not the profit. So memorable.
>
> —John

Another example is in Evanston, Illinois, where the oldest urban commune in the United States is located. It's called the Reba Place Fellowship, after the name of the street. It was founded by Menno-nites, and it's very famous. They live in houses as individual families, but they meet collectively and eat collectively. Some of them have very prominent jobs in terms of income, but their agreement is they will all live on the amount of money that the welfare system defines as poverty. And they have done that for about fifty years now. They bring in so much more money from their jobs than they need to live on that they must, as a community, decide what to do with the excess. They do not invest it in the usual sense. Instead, they buy houses to expand the community.

The Reba Place Fellowship is a community that collectively faces the question, with full intention and purpose: How do we use money? We are seeing this happen in other neighborhood efforts, in the same spirit, with other assets. One example: A neighborhood group went door to door on a couple of blocks in a lower-income neighborhood asking people what they knew well enough to teach young people. On average, people responded with four things that they knew well enough that they could teach. People mentioned things like motorcycle repair. Fishing. Cooking. And also things like how to be kind to others.

So in a two-person household, you would have eight teachables. If there are thirty houses on the block, you have 240 teachables. Let's say there's a school on the next block. Imagine the curriculum that the people on the block could provide. If you saw their gifts in terms of what they knew how to teach and then you looked at the curriculum in the schools, think how offerings from the school could be enhanced by what's on the block next to it.

Thinking this way, we open ourselves to an understanding of the gifts that are already present all around us. We begin to say our future and our productivity are related to this abundance of gifts, previously unrecognized and unused. We might call it a gift economy. We don't have a school problem today; we have a village problem. We have a village of teachers who are not teaching. When we imagine something like a gift economy, we begin building the commons and building a culture.

THE NEIGHBORLY WAY

Which of these three, do you think, was a neighbor. . .? The one who showed him mercy.

—Luke 10:36

The market ideology has its sacraments whereby economics is raised to a spiritual practice. The Dow Jones Industrial Average has become a sacrament of modern times. As has the measure of Gross Domestic Product. Other sacraments are new housing starts. Capital equipment backorders and inventory. Inflation and interest rates. Economic growth. These are the lead stories, front page and business page.

That liturgy is what is under question when we talk about an alternative to the consumer culture economy. The common good calls for communal disciplines and neighborly practices and habits that have everything to do with connectedness and setting up some ground rules for neighborliness and covenant.

When we talk about a more communal life, we do not literally mean a life that is homemade and hand-made. People on the neighborly path are not going to weave their own clothes, even though that's what you see in some alternative economies. Part of what is happening is the demonetization—or you might say the lesser commodification—of life. This, too, needs its rituals, liturgy, ways of keeping track.

Time-banking pioneer Edgar Cahn (1992) talks about an economy of generosity and having a bank account for generous acts. This account becomes a form of sacrament. There is a Community Connections group in Cleveland that holds a fair every Friday night. They get together, they eat, and then each person stands up and says, "This is what I need next week. And this is what I have to offer. And here's the invitation I want to make for the following week or two weeks." They are creating social structures of exchange that are not monetized; it's a liturgy.

The Cleveland gathering is convened by Tom O'Brien. He works for a foundation, which is quite a signpost to the shift afoot. Foundations have traditionally funded only the regular social services and the high-end fine arts. The Cleveland Foundation decided to do something for grassroots people. For ten years it has spent five million dollars making grants. They don't like being identified as being as a conventional grant-maker so they use the grants as an attractor. They have started two thousand projects over a ten-year period, one of which is the Friday-night gathering in Cleveland where people exchange gifts. They are building social fabric and neighborly habits.

A more communal life comes to be when a group of citizens, over time, decides what they have to invent to build a neighborhood. In this way, neighborhood connections become a movement. This is how culture is created.

Another example: National People's Action, an association of local community groups, assembles in Washington every year. People from neighborhoods all across the country come, and after all their business activities, they have a big party. At the height of the party, the oldest person there, Otto, would stand up and say, "I'm going to tell you our story." And then he would go back to the beginning of the organization and its story. And all the new people who had come to the meeting knew that, in that evening and at that place where there was food and drink and singing, they had come into a community culture. They knew its past and its ways.

That's what a culture manifests: a way of being. Otto stood up and told the story every year because the organization had new people coming in and they had to know the association's story, its particular "our way." What Otto stood for was memory. Living memory. And history. Knowing those upon whose shoulders we stand. So that's one part of culture: storytelling. It's a secular sacrament.

Culture can be the atmosphere in a room and with certain high-engagement practices, you can see and feel a shift. If you want to know how to create an atmosphere that supports kindness, it's simple: Put people in real contact with each other. In a two-hour period people connect in small groups. You see their faces change. You see their bodies relax. You see the smiles in their eyes. In a short time they are treating each other with a kindness and warmth that didn't exist when you began. It is quick, low cost, and—pardon the term—scalable.

THE ALTERNATIVE TO RESTLESS PRODUCTIVITY

Even the stork in the heavens knows its times, and the turtledove, swallow, and crane observe the time of their coming; but my people do not know the ordinance of the Lord.

—Jeremiah 8:7

The local living and cooperative movement makes the dominant culture very, very nervous. They will say that constructing practices and disciplines without the safety of a predictable economic path is subsistence living, which is considered to be "undeveloped." Primitive. Pre-modern. Now we see people growing their own food, getting their clothing from a clothing exchange, joining co-operatives.

What supports the idea of neighborliness is that there is a generation now that cannot get on the market track. We have prosperity without jobs. And we have younger people who want something more than a career. Their concerns are about a set of values, a balanced life, an alternative life, a different way of handling productivity and making a living. Not moving around. Or moving up.

This means we need not despair over the unemployment picture and the economic indexes. What we see in our neighbors is a shift in consciousness given expression by a shift in the kind of economy that they are living into. Our children won't be as wealthy as we are. That's just fine. They will be healthier. They will live in a local economy where they aren't working for a global institution. They might work waiting tables. They are spending some time creating craftworks and starting local co-operatives. They are part of a community agriculture process in which they enjoy growing crops and eating healthy food. They are starting small businesses.

This is a ripening of the culture, and we are as nervous about it as we are because it is not safe or predictable. That is why the business sections of media do not call this news. But that's part of taking the alternative path; it is the modern form of going into the wilderness. An off-market journey.

This path is going to happen anyway. The question of where we are now in terms of the mainline track is based on the reality that we can produce goods and services with fewer and fewer people. John has a friend who is an economist who said to him: "John, you value work, and every economist thinks labor is a disability. We need to get rid of workers. Everything we do is to get rid of workers. This has been the track to success." We are to the place where there are such efficiencies in the system in the commodity world that we can produce an overwhelming variety of stuff with many, many fewer people. That is why the market is always trying to create new needs.

This is the future we are all facing. Even college graduates are would-be workers in a system that does not need them. Ivan Illich wrote a book years ago called *The Right to Useful Unemployment* (1978), which was concerned with the activities by which people are useful to themselves and others outside the production of commodities for the market. What we are facing as a society is exploring the question of what useful unemployment is. If I'm not going to be a part of the market production empire, what is my way?

This is a paradigm shift, away from depending on institutions to depending on associational life, the local life that was discovered in the wilderness of the Old Testament. In Old Testament terms, the work is to welcome the widow and the orphan and the immigrant. The modern language is welcoming people on the margin. These actions are pivotal. If we talk about a covenantal community, there is at bottom only one question: How do we treat the widow and the orphan and the immigrant? This becomes an organizing principle of an alternative narrative. And it begins with a series of covenants.

A key covenant is to see the gifts of the widow. And the orphan. And the immigrant. Anyone on the margin. We were all there once. People of any prosperity or power are always surprised when the gifts of those that they blame or look down on are revealed. This exposure of gifts is the way into the kind of community that we want. It's one of the most significant acts that we can do.

We find this hospitality nearer than we think. It is the custom of well-off schools to send their students on field trips to Africa or Latin America. The students always find the same thing. They say, "We went into the poorest hut, in the poorest neighborhood, in the poorest township, and those people had light in their eyes. They had smiles on their faces, and they welcomed us."

The instinct that creates these trips is sincere, but these are imperial journeys. We do not have to travel afar to find light, and smiles, and gifts. They are always within walking distance, in a nearby place that we are simply unaccustomed to visiting.

THE SHADOW SIDE OF COMMUNITY

There are also limits to the local life. Cultures have a shadow side. They can be dark, confining, and unkind. They don't forgive. They shun. They stone.

A focus on local can lead to parochialism. It can produce the tribalism that results in constant warfare, as in the history that we know. One of the positive things one might say about the empire is that it has often stopped warfare. It brought peace, like Pax Britannica, to quell the dangers of parochialism. As we seek the communal culture, we must come to grips with this problem: Perhaps our focus on the local will also bring with it divisiveness, its own kind of competition, some form of warfare.

One of the downsides of small communities is un-welcoming-ness, drawing the boundary against outsiders. You could live somewhere for ten years, and you're still not really a member. Exclusive cultures are a part of our wish for certainty. They have much of what we seek—ritual, memory, habits of connection. But there is a difference between useful habits and fundamentalism. The certainty of fundamentalism leads to violence. This is often laid at the feet of the poor in the world. It is also a fear that the values of our cultures are disappearing, and so we gather in tribal enclosures.

When communities come to power—even communities of covenant—they begin to formulate self-predictive rules. In the religious traditions what you get are rules of holiness that right away begin to stratify people and organize people and administer people so that you are soon back on the system track. The point is, even the neighborly way requires great intentionality because it regularly is distorted by the seductive power of control. The Church, even with its covenantal language and well-meaning, went through a phase in the 1990s you could call a big-church growth movement; the ideology was that you could grow a bigger church because people like homogenous assemblages. So you gather all the people who are alike. It works. Witness the mega-churches—global, prosperous, and like-minded.

Walter was on a program with representatives from the Episcopal House of Bishops and the author of *The Big Sort,* a stunning data-filled book documenting the move in America toward our own kind (Bishop, 2009). The Bishops were worried that their Dioceses were turning red or blue. That's the thesis of *The Big Sort*: People now move into neighborhoods of like-minded people. Mobility is the modern vehicle for encouraging exclusive communities, at every economic level, and we are becoming ever more homogenous.

There is no real way around this aspect of our humanity. We hope for forgiveness and hospitality, but there is too much evidence they are in short supply. Small communities, traditionally, have dilemmas and always will. The consumer culture did not create original sin. The point is, there's nothing in what we're saying that gets rid of any human weaknesses. Departing the consumer culture is just changing the context. It's believing that a context of cooperation and concern for the commons will increase the likelihood of welcome and forgiveness.

6

THE
DISCIPLINES OF
NEIGHBORLINESS

It is more blessed to give than to receive.

—Acts 20:35

The sacred texts have stood the test of time. The sieve that those stories have been sifted through for so long is what makes them valid. In community work, the sacred text has to be joined with the language of neighbor for it to have any power. Otherwise, neighborliness becomes a utilitarian project and the sacred texts become an intellectual exercise, spoken to near empty chapels. What good is it to be neighbors if what that means is to make life a little easier, lower cost, more convenient? The community work is to practice the neighborly disciplines, to celebrate the secular sacraments of neighborliness.

We are accustomed to the disciplines that belong to faith; there also are disciplines that belong to community. They are built by covenantal language held together by vow rather than barter and honor the fact that community has a job to do and needs to be productive. They are the way to covenantal justice, the way we get people to participate or engage in a more just society and a more sustainable earth.

Some signposts of an alternative social order of a society organized around covenantal promises sustaining the common good are:

- *Time.* Space for relatedness and hospitality to be chosen as alternatives to speed, individualism, and like-mindedness.
- *Food.* Choosing to grow food locally, urban farms, food without chemical intervention, food as the sacred table around which culture and community are sustained and created.
- *Silence.* Quieting the noise of the automated, electronic, consumption-as-entertainment culture. Silence as a means of honoring mystery. Listening as an action step. An opening for the voice of nature and neighbor. Creating a place for thought and depth. A quality of Sabbath and reflection as an answer to restless productivity and advertising.

Time, food, and silence are three major disciplines for creating the conditions for neighborliness and producing social re-ordering. Those disciplines recognize the human condition, which the hubris of our market culture denies. They go against the grain of a culture of productivity, consumption, speed, entertainment, barter, and amnesia.

Each discipline is a manifestation of, and supported by, *covenant*, a belief in *abundance*, and *ritual*. Covenant is holding a relationship sacred. Traditionally, it meant with God or a higher power. Here it is about our relationships with neighbors and even strangers. It means holding community and the commons sacred; it requires honoring vows as an expression of both freedom and fidelity. Abundance faces the questions of our relationship to money, the right use of wealth, and the reconstruction of money and market, including forgiving our debts, reducing debt slavery, and limiting usury, making money on money. By *ritual* we mean the re-performance of a set of liturgy, memory, and story that brings into the present all that is held precious. Remembering ourselves, putting limbs and body together, through common practices born of knowledge of what it means to be human.

We offer in these neighborly disciplines a way to support the process of reconstructing our social order. They change the way we experience community and make space for the commons.

TIME

In the neighborly way, time is measured by depth and there is enough. No need to rush.

A TIME FOR ALL THINGS

Traditional societies are filled with rituals and celebrations that grow from the annual sequence of life and nature—Mexico has more than 150 days of celebration that trace the year's seasonal progression. Rituals and celebrations are signposts to say we live in this time of year, we are in a circle of time; they are ways for people to find their lives connected to the natural flow of life.

The biggest shift in consciousness is away from thinking, "I don't have time." So much of our traveling is still in the time-is-running-out world. Busyness, or lack of time, is the common argument against Democracy. Oscar Wilde said he was for Socialism, but it took too many evening meetings.

TIME IS THE DEVIL

In the high-tech world, speed is God and time is the devil. Speed becomes a value in itself, a measure of success, winning, and sophistication. Having time is always anti-system. The market engine does everything it can to overcome the time it takes for nature to make something grow: There is today such a thing as the twelve-day tomato.

People living outside the consumer ideology have a different relationship with time. It moves more slowly. The clock has no meaning to many people living on the margin, or in a subsistence culture or a more traditional society. Being on time is not the point. In west Africa, if the bus shows up within twenty-four hours, it is an on-time departure. In community work, you never know when someone is going to show up or not, and when they do, you say, "Welcome. You made it. Good."

Time, then, is a social construction. In an alternative construction of time, people bide their time. They have time on their hands. Like observing the Sabbath, their interpretation of time is an act of defiance against the dominant culture and its restless productivity. The Sabbath gave form to the fact that, no matter how busy I am, there is always time. The lesson from the margins is that there is enough time. In the consumer society time is a scarcity.

In the sacred texts, there is that famous idea in Ecclesiastes: a time to laugh and a time to cry, a time to live and a time to die. In other words, in the seasons there are rhythms that belong to the very structure of creation that cannot be violated with impunity. And they do not necessarily occur by the clock.

The common construction of time was a necessity of the British Navy—that's how the time zones were set up. Pope Gregory earlier, out of concern for stabilizing the date of Easter, solved the problem of how long a day and a year were. We lost enough minutes a year from this that they constructed the idea of the leap year, the extra day in February every four years. Now the Gregorian calendar is what we live by. It was invented for Easter, and became useful for commerce. But the reality is that it was made up.

When did Time become Money? You can say that the whole modern world of productivity required the regimentation of time. One example was establishing Greenwich Mean Time, so that ships of the British Navy could calculate their position anywhere on the water. And then there are the timelines for productivity and the quotas that come with that for the workforce—everything is regimented. As a communal discipline, it is unregimented time that allows for human possibility to emerge.

The usual argument against the neighborly way is that we don't have time for that. We have no time to be with our neighbor. Time has become the incarnation of scarcity. No time is always the argument against collaboration, collectivism, participation, democracy. "We don't have time for that" is the universal refusal, along with no money. Time and money are regimented and made scarce—and made up, and therefore amenable to transformation.

STANDING IN LINE

My times are in your hand.

—Psalm 31:15

Edd Conboy is the director of social services at the Broadway Ministry in Philadelphia. He noticed the people from the street coming to Broadway's food kitchen spent most of their time waiting in line. Soon he began to realize that their standing in line was a measure of the consumer culture's elitism and privilege. In the market world the privileged do not wait in line; they have priority access and reserved first-class seats. The poor and the homeless wait in line all the way around the block. The elite do not queue up. At fundraisers for not-for-profits, the donors never have to wait. They go to the front of the line, while the "normal" people wait in a line that wraps around the corner. Not at Edd's place.

Edd found a way to eliminate all waiting lines at his church. First, he set up round tables with cloth tablecloths and real silverware. Then, he invited everyone, as soon as they showed up, to be seated. The volunteers served the tables. Welcome to our restaurant, they said. Once you decide to restructure the social order, there are a thousand ways to do it: Rearranging the room or the space and finding ways to serve everyone at the same time are just the beginning.

KAIROS

Before farming became so scientific, good farmers were embedded in a culture and tradition that taught knowledge about the soil, the seasons, the way to plant. They developed a sense of when it was the right time to do anything. There was a time to care for the land, so you had a sense of the future. Part of the Old Testament Jubilee Year, the year of forgiveness, is to give the land a rest.

Time measured by depth is an enemy of the market. The market is sold on the basis of speed and convenience. There are some concessions; for example, for historic reasons the stock market closes on Good Friday.

In the New Testament a great deal is made out of an alternative word for time: *Kairos*. Jungian therapy talks about Kairos and Kronos, Kronos being tick-tock time and Kairos meaning time measured by depth. In the Bible Kairos is an explosive moment of extreme significance. In the struggle against Apartheid the churches of South Africa put together what is famously called the Kairos Document, a declaration of the faith community's stance: "This is the moment." More recently, there is a Kairos Document produced by the Palestinians that says: "This is the moment of grace and opportunity." Both are examples of time measured by significance.

Our work is to declare that this is the time to accelerate the conversation about alternatives to the market ideology. Even though there may not be demand for it for ten years or fifty years. This is the moment.

This is the right time. There is a time for certain things that you can't calendarize, which means you can't make them predictable. You can't control them. So time has its own way with us. This creates the necessity of rethinking time. Re-understanding time is a critical step to get onto the path.

FOOD

As a discipline of neighborliness, food is produced and prepared locally. Sharing and consuming food is a slow and sacred occasion.

The commodification by the market occurs most visibly in our food. It is fast, highly processed, and all vegetables are available all year long. Fast food replaces memory. It replaces affection. It has separated the family and marked the end of the family meal, the family dinner. Plus, it is unhealthy and not appetizing. We are willing to sacrifice our health and enjoyment for so-called convenience. For speed and to save time. Domino's Pizza, the originator of the thirty-minute delivery guarantee, holds an annual contest in which its pizza-making employees from all over the United States compete to see who can make the fastest pizza. Not the tastiest . . . the fastest.

The covenantal community relies on slow and sacred food: bread, wine. That's one reason why food is one of the neighborly disciplines. Food also signifies a space for table prayers. Giving thanks before you eat is an acknowledgement that the food is a gift and not property or an achievement or a possession. As a discipline of neighborly covenant, food is a regular concrete re-performance of gratitude.

FOOD AND SACRED RE-PERFORMANCE

Extend hospitality to strangers.

—Romans 12:13

The potlatch of the indigenous peoples of the Pacific Northwest was a way of gift-giving that "mimics how nature gives without expectation and with rich abundance flourishing" (Anielski, 2015). This is the basis of the communal dinners we call potlucks. Think also of wedding dinners. Thanksgiving. Harvest feasts. *We will eat together. Could you bring some food?* And singing and dancing. All communal disciplines. And all very much a form of sacramental activity.

These customs are examples of re-performance, a repeated act of the normative narrative that is done with great imaginative generativity. The Super Bowl is a re-performance of market ideology: It inculcates us into consumerism. Another example is the evening news, which socializes us into the danger around us and thus the need for protection and caution. It reminds us that no one is safe without the protection of Pharaoh, empire, and public safety. Table prayers before we share food at the table are a re-performance of original gratitude. Re-performance is always an act of socialization.

The Church says the Last Supper was its founding institutionalizing event. It was part of Christ's constructing an alternative future. Constructing the Church and the religious institutions. Constructing His legacy. Whether or not Christ saw it that way, that's what the Church says, so it is the meal that we continue to re-perform and replicate. Every time we do that, we can re-imagine ourselves back on that Thursday in that dangerous room, except that now we've got so many layers of stuff on top of its significance that it's hard to notice that re-performance is what we are doing.

The Last Supper is certainly in continuity with the Jewish practice of the Passover Seder, the annual ritual by which Jewish families or communities retell the story of the Israelites' Exodus from slavery in Egypt. The

Last Supper in the Christian tradition becomes the way of re-performing that meal of intimacy. And in the Gospel of Luke, when Jesus makes a Resurrection appearance to the two disciples who don't know who he is, the text says Jesus was known to them in the breaking of the bread, which is an allusion to the Eucharist, the Body of Christ. So it was the meal itself that made present the neighbor they most valued.

This calls us to reinstitute the family dinner, which the market has reduced to takeout, pre-prepared meals, eating in motion, eating according to the schedule of restless productivity. A great New York preacher, George Buttrick, once said that, in Manhattan, the Church is the only place where the great estate owners and their butlers met together at a table. Every food table, festival, community gathering has that possibility.

> One of the best neighborhood organizations I have known over the years was in Chicago. It had meetings once a month, but they weren't really meetings; they were potluck suppers where people talked about their issues and their possibilities. From the meal emerged the dialogue, and the vision. Compared to the meetings of most neighborhood groups, this was a transforming reality: the movement from potluck to dialogue to vision.
>
> —John

A different kind of sacred food is the soul food that your mother fixed. At some point in time, a crisis of being newly married is when you discover that your spouse doesn't fix the food that your mother fixed. And so that has to be negotiated. But soul food from home feels like you are in the place where you belong. In the Christian tradition, the bread and the wine are the very particular soul food that is embedded in a particular narrative. And so every priest and minister recites the same narrative for the night that Jesus was betrayed. You cannot homogenize or universalize that. It belongs to a remembered place, in a ritual that can be re-performed. It cannot occur quickly, or at the mall, or while driving.

THE LOCAL FOOD MOVEMENT

Fast food and supermarket processed food are foundational to the market ideology. There is an awakening to this. Every city is now proud of its community gardens, of its co-ops, of its small farms and ranches nearby. Restaurants now brand themselves by using local suppliers. Another sign the transformation is occurring.

The co-operative movement is at the center, especially with food. Co-ops are a major form of production returning to the community. When we shop for vegetables that are locally grown many of them are ugly. They are not all cleaned up and polished and packaged. This is a prime example of a handmade and local economy at work. Not perfect-looking carrots, but just right.

What is important in the local food movement is that we are experiencing practices that support community. When we imagine a future that nurtures aliveness, it comes in the form of the producer and consumer having an intimate relationship with each other. What is appealing about any local market is not just the local circulation of money, but also the relationship of mutual accountability that says, "We are creating this community and the commons together."

FOOD AND CULTURE

A culture is language, food, faith, art, all intertwined. Food is always a critical component. Food that grows with culture is food that is local. So that people like the Inuit developed a food that was their communal food. The Mayans did the same, but developed a foodway based on what was around them, in their world. Through time their ability to produce their own food from what was local also provided them with healthful ways of eating and living, learned from their past.

Think of the Mediterranean diet that has been designated as a life-producing or heart-attack-diminishing diet. The Mediterranean diet isn't a diet that somebody thought up; it was eating what grows in the Mediterranean region. It was a way to use the things that grew there and prepare them in a proliferation of tasty ways. What the empire has done is, first, to break us from a foodway that comes from our place and is healthful and, then, substitute a completely artificial way of feeding ourselves. And one of the results of that has a name: obesity. It is the mark of a people broken from the food of their place.

The commodified system world is powerfully embodied in food. When misfortune occurs, it becomes a marketing opportunity. Drought, pestilence, crop-loss—none of it matters. From the agri-business point of view, those events are localized and there's plenty of production somewhere else to supply the fast-food purveyors and fill the supermarkets. Cost goes up, but profits are intact, and customers are not inconvenienced.

That's how the supermarket offers you more choice at a lower cost. Its low-cost food gives the illusion of freedom, and that may be why the commitment to growing and eating local food makes such a difference.

In a market economy, a food company is only interested in food that they can process, food to which they can add ingredients for appearance and shelf life. You can't make money off lettuce. You can't make money from a pork chop. You can't make money off milk. When you go into a supermarket all of the commodities we all need—the dairy, the meat, the produce—are on the perimeter and at the back of the store to draw you through the aisles of processed food, where all the profit margin is. Agri-business almost gives away the lettuce and the tomatoes. And they will fight each other over space for the processed food and the non-food items.

The supermarket is the construction, and the epicenter, of the commodity world. The food movement tells you to be healthy. It tells you to only eat what your grandmother would have cooked. Food that rots. But supermarket food dominates the landscape. Processed food produces shelf life and appearance. It's all about economics, and the only way you can make money is by adding value. The food companies would argue that they are adding value with their processing methods. They claim to have good ingredients, but they modify them to add sweetness, prolong shelf life, and lower costs. Saying processed food is healthy food is right up there with dentists claiming that electrifying a toothbrush to move up and down faster is adding value.

We hold similar beliefs about our bodies. We think that the path to health is diet and exercise; that's market discipline applied to our bodies, our health. The documentary *Fed Up* exposes the most colonizing idea that ever existed: that the goal of the diet industry is marketing the belief that fewer calories and more exercise are somehow related to your health. The documentary's assertion is that diet and exercise have little to do with your health, or obesity. The major factor affecting health and obesity, it says, is the amount of sugar you take in every day. And if you look on any label at the percentages of daily dietary requirements a product provides, you will see that the percentage for sugar is never listed. The food processing industry has lobbied Congress and the FDA to leave that detail blank because it would tell you that this little candy bar or that can of soda has 700 percent more sugar than you need in a day.

In its focus on diet and exercise, the health care industry is promising immortality. An answer to mystery. In a market world, selling diet and exercise as the keys to the kingdom promotes the idea that I have the capacity to live forever. Simply trust our products.

What is our alternative? You might say that one is the Mediterranean diet. But the Mediterranean diet is a part of a culture. It represents stuff in a place that people have learned to use through time, in a very appetizing way. So don't eat processed food. Eat only those things that rot. Processed food is immortal, despite the fact that it carries an expiration date. It's always a year ahead of time, so you're eating something that's going to sit on that shelf for a year.

To participate in a communal world and covenantal culture is to be conscious about food. The alternative is for us, in the place where we are, to construct life practices and work practices that embody this thing called exercise and diet. The communal culture will embody it. Your body will be engaged in a way that it won't grow fat. And the food you eat will similarly be enhancing your body. This is a cultural discipline. It has low profit margins, but you can sell your food-related stocks as a beginning ritual.

SILENCE

But about that day or hour no one knows.

—Matt. 24:36

Silence is a companion of mystery, and listening is its fellow traveler. The first thing to say is that the central word of Judaism is *Shema*: Hear, O, Israel. So Israel is a listening people, and when it does not listen it ceases to be Israel because it falls out of Covenant. Listening puts you in a receptive mode. Being receptive requires you to celebrate Sabbath. Sabbath is a season of receptivity. The commodity system wants you never to be in a receptive mode. It wants you to be in an assertive mode. To sell or acquire. To listen is really to retreat from the commodity system, to retreat from productivity. A form of Sabbath.

LISTENING

On the election of Cardinal Jorge Bergoglio as Pope, the conventional wisdom was that in choosing the last two Popes the electors had picked the smartest guy in the room. The question for the 2013 conclave became: Can they pick a guy who will listen to the other people in the room?

Think of how the market culture keeps us from listening to the slow food and local living movement: They are continually relegated to anomalies in the free market consumer ideology. The result is that we can't easily hear the neighborly story. It is a human interest story, told once. Just as an addicted person can't hear the world of sobriety, the neighborly story is there, but we can't hear it. And so neighborliness could be an opening of the ears. How do we come to hear that call? What are the attractors? We see the seduction that leads to the addiction, but it's more useful to ask what we have in common that could be called to so that people would finally hear.

We have ancient stories that tell us about the value of silence. We have modern stories that come out of our lives and our experience that tell us the value of quiet. There are cultures that embody it. The Catholic Church has its contemplative orders like the Trappist monks and the cloistered nuns of the Visitation Order who exemplify the virtue of silence in performing their work and expressing their relationship with God. In Buddhism and other meditative traditions, silence is essential to transforming the mind and using it to explore itself and other phenomena.

QUAKERS AND TIME AND LISTENING

Historically, the Quakers were people who had a culture in which time and silence and welcome were embodied in their communal experience. They are a good example of a people with a culture that manifests a different use of time and silence. Their most notable public presence is their activism around peace. If we started out with a question like "How do we achieve peace?" we could look to the Quakers, observe the culture they come from, and see that it includes a large space for quiet time to be together and to welcome all. The welcoming spirit, the quiet, the space to be together—these things combine to build a community with characteristics that evoke peace. The Reverend A.J. Muste, the great pacifist, said there is no way to peace, peace is the way. When we ask "What is the culture that evokes kindness?" we are not looking for kind people in a community, we are looking for a community that calls for kindness. So in talking about the Quakers we are talking about a community that calls for peace, which comes from the practice of time together and silence and listening.

That's an example of the difference between us being in a room together and being on the phone together. On the phone, it's almost impossible to allow silence: *Hello, are you there? Can you hear me now?* "Can you hear me now?" expresses our anxiety about silence, our fear that there's nobody out there. That there's no God.

Silence is also an act of useful unemployment. Silence is made obsolete in a plugged-in world. Plugging in is a form of privatization. It is a substitute for silence. It claims to promote connection. When young people in the midst of a conversation with you are texting with a phone in each hand, who are they talking to?

SACRAMENTS OF SILENCE

The practice of listening brings people together. It reminds us that we are not alone. When people gather, the right questions bring the sacred into the room—questions of connections, not opinions. If you bring questions of depth, questions that are personal, the experience of being together shifts. When we ask questions that are an invitation to hear each other, something is created. The Quakers understand this.

How do you construct ways to listen to each other? One is to present questions that evoke profound speech versus just talk. Any time you ask a question that results in a list, nothing is going to happen. Questions of analysis are interesting but not powerful. The questions you ask have to take you into conversations of doubt, fallibility, confession, mystery, and apology. For example, you ask people, "What's the crossroad you are at in this stage of your life?" Every time you do that—you can do it in a group of a thousand—the room changes.

It doesn't even matter if they don't answer the question. The question itself has force, spiritual force. It creates a clearing. It enables people to hold open the space for listening and depth. A good question always initiates this. Good questions can be considered as sacraments of silence.

COVENANT: A VOW OF FREEDOM AND FAITHFULNESS

God stands as someone who would make a Covenant. Covenant is not required in the market world. It is central to the language of the community and commons. The neighborly world understands this. It becomes an underpinning for an alternative economy. A covenant is a vow. A contract tries to capture and define everything. Every word and every possibility. But a covenant has much more meaning. It's open-ended. It is a continuing exercise of freedom in faithfulness. It is so hard to hold faithfulness and freedom together, because freedom without faithfulness becomes autonomy. And faithfulness without freedom becomes an obligation, a legalism. To have both is the point.

The sixteenth century Anabaptists chose to live outside the codes of dominant culture, which is why they were endlessly persecuted. They were an extraordinary social countermovement in that they did not adhere to the norms of the empire or the nation state.

The Anabaptists believed in adult baptism rather than infant baptism. In the sixteenth century, infant baptism was essentially the pathway to membership in the state. And adult baptism had to do with being old enough to decide that you would be under the disciplines of Christ and not under the disciplines of state—adult baptism was a dissenting activity, an incredible act of defiant freedom.

But it also was a move to say that in this community you have to be conscious of your choice, and infant baptism does not allow that. It is the choice of the parents. The choice made for you. The unforgettable lesson from the Anabaptists is this: Freedom—from an economic system and the dominant culture—is a choice available to all. When that choice is supported by a religious community . . . powerful and rare.

COVENANT AND RETRIBUTIVE JUSTICE

The market ideology demands uncovenantal justice. The sanctity of private property and contracts require retributive justice: eye for an eye, three strikes and you're out, failure is not an option. The alternative is restorative justice, which is covenantal, not contractual.

Retributive means you get what's coming to you. Retribution. Contrast this with covenantal justice. The widely used term is "distributive justice," as contrasted to retributive justice. Not restorative, but distributive. Distributive means the wealth of the community is distributed equitably across the community, wealth in this case being justice based on all being members of the community, members by the fact of their being human beings. Distributive justice is designed with and according to the requirements of the commons, the common good.

ABUNDANCE AND THE RIGHT USE OF MONEY

Money has utility, and we need disciplines that encourage the economy but embody covenant. This means we need to change our relationship with money. It is not the source of all evil; we have just constructed it so. It is not money, but the abuse of money that is the problem.

The neighborhood or community needs its connection to the larger world, and money is the language for this connection. This point of view is not about being self-sufficient. It does mean we do what we can locally. We can grow our own food, in urban and rural communities, and keep much of the production and exchange local.

There are inventions that support a covenantal neighborhood. One example is local currencies. BerkShares are one kind of currency that gives a five percent discount at local merchants who have agreed to accept them. Local citizens exchange ninety-five Federal dollars for one hundred BerkShares at participating banks, then spend them at full value at participating businesses. Businesses can recirculate them with other local businesses at full value or take them back to any of the eight branches of the banks and exchange them back into Federal dollars at a five percent discount. The merchants can afford to do this because they know that if they keep this money local they are going to thrive.

The inspiration for later local currency initiatives was the "Constant," issued by Ralph Borsodi in 1972 in Exeter, New Hampshire. The Constant was tied in value to a standard basket of commodities, so it held a steady purchasing value, contrary to national currencies. And contrary to myth, Borsodi was never arrested by Federal agents. In fact, when a reporter asked the FBI if the Constant was illegal, the response was, "We don't care if he is issuing acorns as long as they do not look like Federal dollars." Counterfeiting is illegal—but not the local issue of currency.

Borsodi wanted something behind his currency that was stable in value so that the huge inflationary pressure and variation of the stock market could be avoided. This is what communities need. They need a currency that frees them from the complete control of the banking system. We need Federal currency to deal with the outside world, but we want to balance that dependency.

North Dakota is the only state with a state bank, and they have dampened the major swings of recession and inflation because that state controls and issues its own debt; it controls the issue of money. In hard times, the Bank of North Dakota pours money in, and it doesn't incur any interest expense because private banking is out of the equation. It doesn't pay interest. This is important. What weighs most heavily on the national economy is the interest on the national debt, not the principal. Forty percent of the deficit in the United States is pure interest on the debt (Brown, 2012). And we owe it to the private sector because we are afraid to turn banks into utilities. The Federal Reserve is owned by the private sector. North Dakota, since 1919, has avoided this.

In addition to these local ventures, we still will have to deal with the larger economic and credit systems. Student loans are a clear example of being out of balance with money. The private sector got into this business and, in the name of free enterprise, has saddled our youth with huge debt. When you borrow from the government for a student loan, you can do things to have it forgiven. You can give two years of your life to public service, for example, and the debt is forgiven. You borrow from the private bank and there is no forgiveness.

Money and Our Affection for Place

In the modern world, the idea of the "free" economy has falsely associated freedom with going where the money dictates. Covenant and community rely on an affection for what is local and near, a regard for "this place." Residents who stay for a while, associational life, street life, a memory, children who can walk more than a block from their house are things every neighborhood needs.

Central to all of this is some form of a nearby business district. Nearby companies to find work. Community is not just thinking of our block and neighbors; a community can't perform its functions without a local economy. You will not have a local economy unless people care about the place. Unless we have some affection for our community, we are not going to shop, nearby or not, to keep the money at home.

A Liturgy for the Common Good

A liturgy is a regularly performed script that in performance promises to transform. It is more powerful than a map because a map pretends that there's a destination that we can know about it. In Christian tradition, some liturgical elements are praise, confession, thanksgiving, dedication. Thanksgiving includes collecting money. Then dedication, at the end of the liturgy, means you're supposed to commit again. This is the construction of the worship service.

Neighborliness is the opportunity to be aware every day that we are performing an alternative liturgy. To know that my life is either the performance of a deathly liturgy, or the possibility of something alive. A liturgy of aliveness. A liturgy in favor of the common good. The people who write in liturgy are always fond of beginning by saying that, etymologically speaking, the meaning of the word *liturgy* is work. They say that liturgy is the work of the people. So is the work of generating the common good.

PROPHETIC POSSIBILITIES

The practice of memory of a narrative in a place generates prophecy. Prophets are artistic voices that arise out of communal practice and speak to the possibilities and to the distortions. It is always easier to talk about the distortions than it is to talk about the possibilities, but the prophets always talk about both. The way the Hebrew Bible is put together, when the prophets appear, they arise out of the Torah. So the Torah is that liturgical practice of the memory out of which these peculiar artistic personalities arise.

The liturgy holds the prophecy over time. It becomes the order of service. It is a network of symbols that yield a world. In neighborliness, it is a counter-world because in the market world the liturgy is a commodity liturgy. The orgies of the Super Bowl and Black Friday are concrete re-performances of scarcity (winning is everything), violence (at the line of scrimmage), acquisition (I shop, therefore I am), and reverence for the market ideology (both are the lead news stories of the day).

> I went to a Reds game a while back, and before the game sixteen couples were married. In the ballpark. They had a podium and a minister. Some of them were dressed conventionally for a wedding, but some of them had baseball uniforms on. Maybe they get married in a ballpark because they love baseball. But it's clear they also wanted something showy and modern. It's an expression of the Super Bowl mentality.
>
> —Walter

Required in the face of the market liturgy are subversive liturgies to say that the dominant culture is not as all-powerful as it is. This is not a new idea. All of the religions of the Book have counter-liturgies that call to a different order of communal resistance.

At that Thursday dinner before the Crucifixion, Jesus said, "Now I'm going to tell you the final thing I need to tell you. You are no longer servants. You are friends." The problem the Church has had was defined by that sentence. That's the institutional nexus. The prior message had been "servants," and service is a value not to be placed equal to friendship. Service can be commoditized and friendship cannot. The commons and a neighborly culture value friends.

STORY AS LITURGY AND RE-PERFORMANCE

Community is built on the power of story. Story evokes a memory, an affection for place and one another. A group of people with a story has continuity, and their story gives them a sense of uniqueness. At the center of the neighborly liturgy is constantly remembering where we came from. You see this in the efforts at collecting oral history, in the lobbies of libraries and museums, in public spaces, in large city murals.

You know you are in a place that is living the neighborly way when it's explicit about its story. The Hopi Indians in the Black Mesa area of Arizona are the most isolated of all the indigenous tribes; they were forced up there by the Navajo. Each of their eleven villages has a different creation story. Perhaps it is because the Navajo invaded all their lands and forced them together on the Mesa. They didn't come from the same place in the literal sense, and now there they are with eleven stories. The Bible is a story of the whole people together. We rarely have a narrative about our place in most neighborhoods. But when you go to a neighborhood organization meeting and you hear people say, "Do you remember when we did this?" understand that they are building their story.

THE RE-PERFORMING POWER OF LITURGY

In ancient Israel the way they sustained Covenant was to fashion liturgies in which they kept re-performing the founding events and the community's founding memories. In the Church today, the reiteration of the Eucharist is always to perform again Christ's instruction: Do this in remembrance of Me. And of course the Passover observance is the re-performance of the Exodus narrative. Both those liturgies feed the imagination and the identity of the community so that we don't forget the direction we intended to be walking.

But the capacity to sustain that kind of a liturgy is always distorted when the liturgy itself becomes a mode of control. So the Church with its liturgies eventually became exclusionary, and deciding who is qualified to participate in the liturgy emptied it of its generative force.

The Church doesn't have a monopoly on sacramental life, but if you think about the seven sacraments of the Catholic Church, sacramental life is a complete life cycle. The performance of a particular sacrament is to say that the whole energy, the holiness, of life is gathered in this moment for this child or for this couple or this deceased person. The whole universe is gathered around this unique individual at this unique moment.

Serious communities are always developing and sustaining their sacramental practices, which the commodity system cannot possibly do because control is the antithesis of mystery. Serious communities hold block parties, clean-up days, art and music events, Friday gatherings to make requests, offers, and invitations. They survey the gifts of the neighbors. They teach entrepreneurial skills; they shop and spend their dollars locally and close by. They grow food and gardens. They connect the elders with the children and learn the names of these children. They meet once a week to have coffee. They produce a local newsletter or website or newspaper. They affirm and expand associational life.

All these practices are creating a memory of the place. This is not nostalgia for another era. These are sacraments of departure from the consumer culture. They situate human community and human persons in a bottomless mystery—in a mystery where time, silence, imperfection, covenant are elements of the modern, off-market wilderness. An other kingdom.

Everything will be all right in the end . . . if it's not all right, then it's not the end.

—The Best Exotic Marigold Hotel

POSTSCRIPT:
BEYOND MONEY AND CONSUMPTION

After only two verses into the wilderness, the Israelites wanted the food and certainty of Pharaoh. Woody Allen's version of that features two women leaving a restaurant in Miami: One says, "The food was terrible." The other says, "Yes, and the portions were so small." The free market consumer ideology assumption is that we want larger portions of everything that is so unsatisfying. Consumption is the modern version of Pharaoh. Leaving consumption is the fear of our freedom. That is why we need community.

Luckily, there are people helping us resist the return. People who are seriously upending the measures of the current social order. One step is to question the Gross Domestic Product as a measurement of how we are doing and replace it with other measures of well-being. This takes us to measures that speak to the common good. The common good cannot be measured by the total dollars that change hands.

We have TimeBanking. Edgar Cahn (1992) has developed a measure for generosity. He says, "Let's not measure the exchange of money—it's too small, and it is the ultimate commodifying agent. Let's measure good works and call *that* the core economy. When one person spends an hour serving another, that goes in a bank account." TimeBanking is a steppingstone on an alternative path. Cahn is reconstructing an economy. From centers in thirty countries at a time, he is creating a neighborhood economy. And he enlists the capacity of people for whom the market has no use. He calls that co-production (2004). That is a beacon. This replaces Charity: co-production, where benefits accrue to both sides in every exchange.

Mark Anielski (2007) has developed a Genuine Well-Being Index. It replaces the Gross Domestic Product as the measure of success. His book *The Economics of Happiness* joins the movement around the world to create practices that release us from the cultural dominance of the market economy.

On another front, Peter Pula and his colleagues at Axiom News look for stories that have the capacity to give the community life instead of focusing on its woundedness. And Howard Lawrence and the people working with him on the Abundant Community Initiative in Edmonton, Alberta, are transforming a city, one neighborhood at a time.

These innovations are illustrations of the future existing in the present. They are simply examples that guide us to an other kingdom. They are ushering us into a really new era. What seemed radical a few years ago is now all around us. Not yet mainstream, not yet considered very newsworthy, but soon. This is happening not as a utopian dream, but because the market ideology has reached its limits.

TIMING IS EVERYTHING

Our basic intent in writing this book is to shrink the market as the primary means of cultural identity, schools as the sole source of learning, systems as the source of care, price as the measure of value, productivity as the basis for being. This shift will be near the center of the transformation.

Given these aims, we are waiting for a social movement, grassroots action where something is ignited. It's hard to predict what that's going to be. When you think of social change movements, even in hindsight, you ask, Why did that event do it and not that one over there? There are social movements happening now; we just have to see them. And hope they are generative, positive ones.

Almost all modern movements were at some time wide-spread yet invisible, and all of them had a precipitate, a trigger. Even now, it's still a mystery why some precipitating factor is necessary. In the seminal days of the Civil Rights Movement in 1949, John and his colleagues sat-in at the State Street Theater in downtown Chicago because black people were required to sit in the balcony. The push for Civil Rights was there, but it wasn't a movement until four students went to lunch at a dime store in Greensboro, North Carolina. The Women's Movement was there, but not visible until people started reading Betty Friedan's book *The Feminine*

Mystique (1963). The Gay Rights Movement was triggered by the police beating people up in the Stonewall riots in Greenwich Village. The Environmental Movement was triggered by *The Silent Spring* (Carson, 1962) and Earth Day; it just suddenly came to life. The Arab Spring was triggered by one young man burning himself up.

For every one of those movements there were all kinds of experiences and discussions, feelings and groups, but it took something else to set them off and made them visible and connect people in a way they never had been. A Kairos moment?

The great changes and shifts that are really significant hardly ever have been designed intentionally beforehand, or resulted because people were trying to make them happen. When he changed his position on the Civil Rights Act of 1964, Senate Minority Leader Everett Dirksen of Illinois said, "You know, everything we've ever done in Congress we did because it's time had come" (Byrd, 1994).

Lenin rushed through Russia because he thought what he had predicted had begun to happen. He got on top of it and made himself the leader. We are always living in the early moments of movements, and what we are talking about here is exactly that. Something is going to happen because of the growing sense of isolation and the longing for commonality.

SIGNS OF CHANGE

Not long ago Walter was at a conference of 4,000 young Evangelical Christians. Walter is not an Evangelical Christian, he's a Christian. The conference was about justice, and these young people were ready to go. Ready to go where they sensed that the cause of justice required one to be.

What was especially striking about those young people is that they were not thinking about their long-term well-being; they were living in the present. They were asking what's possible now, and what's required of me now, and what can I do now. The assumption seemed to be that if they did what they could the future would eventually be all right. And that looked like a very prophetic stance: seeing how their capacities matched up with what the present requires and out of that extrapolating their futures.

COMMENTARIES

We sent an early version of the book to some colleagues to ask them three questions: (1) What strikes you about the book? What point stands out to you? (2) What do you want to know more about? and (3) What kind of people in your world would find this book useful?

Their comments activated changes in our writing, and we also thought that many of the comments were worthy in their own right. They often said in simpler terms what the book is about. We have gathered these here.

ROBERT INCHAUSTI

Robert Inchausti is the author of five books, including *Subversive Orthodoxy* and *The Ignorant Perfection of Ordinary People*. He edited *The Pocket Thomas Merton* and *Echoing Silence: Thomas Merton on Writing*.

This is a succinct take on our collective neurosis—our perversion of the idea of freedom into a desire to live in isolated imaginary worlds of our own creation and control. Everyone has a Facebook page; every Facebook page a "following," and every following a would-be career. We need a new collective vision and cultural narrative to save us from this runaway megalomania—and this book clearly shows us where the battle-line resides.

You did not try to do too much but rather attend to the big picture: the big lie, the over-arching mistake, the great folly that fuels our anger, alienation, and narcissism. You lift the curse by naming our demons—ferreting out their secret Rumpelstiltskin identities. I particularly liked the short history of consumerism with its list of odd moral and historical "turns." It offered a new way to consider exactly what has transformed all of us into products and "success" stories of one kind or another—however puffed-up and imaginary.

All those who suspect their highest aspirations are being perverted and used against them by men and women of greater personal ambition and psychological sophistication [will find this book useful]. It's a book for rebels, innocents, idealists, and the sick at heart.

CORMAC RUSSELL

Managing director of Nurture Development, faculty member of the Asset-Based Community Development Institute, and author of *Asset-Based Community Development: Looking Back to Look Forward.*

Throughout, [what is striking is] the argument that the ideology of the Free Market dominates our cultural narrative and shapes the way we think about everything is clear. Also the view that the serious challenge to the market ideology strikes right at the heart of that ideology and not just the content and the form the ideology takes.

We are not just left in opposition of the market; this book re-enchants the reader with the commons and community but not in a way that romanticizes community. It's a dance; deeply political and profoundly public. But then to interpret all that within a faith perspective is genius. The way you all have created this narrative seems to me to be potentially attractive to all faiths and none, the invitation back to abundance, fallibility, mystery, and the commonwealth is universal. As I read it I was reminded of the scripture passage Matthew 10:16: "I am sending you out like sheep among wolves. Therefore be as shrewd as snakes and as innocent as doves." This book counsels us in the way of shrewdness and innocence, but also reminds me in any case that innocence is profoundly powerful and consequential.

You all explain how "free" market ideology is the lens through which everyone views the world; through this lens the landscape looks bleak, hence the harmful but ubiquitous notion that we should manage scarcity by means of privatization. You show up the so-called ethic of the marketplace: "for me to win you must lose." And then how you ground this in real-life examples and metaphors, for example, how we learn this maxim from the age of four when we are taught that for me to get an "A" or "B" grade, another kid has to get a "C" or a "D." The market ideology contaminates every aspect of our lives, from the moment of birth onwards. "It is the sea in which we swim."

I also enjoyed the arguments that our politicians are the products of our consciousness. That if we believe we are the "effect" of their decisions and actions, they will become technocratic not democratic. Conversely, if we believe we are the "cause" of our own and, consequently, their actions, they will serve us.

The book challenges the institutional assumption: that institutions and professionals can unilaterally provide us with a good life, and unashamedly points out that it is one of the most anti-democratic notions there is.

What I'd like to know more about is why the three of you choose to write this book? What was your journey? Why you three, why now? What brought you together? What have you learned from each other? In a sense you have created a commonwealth of your lives' journey, and that's a story worth sharing in my opinion.

I also find myself wondering about the route home, back to community and back to the commons, the prodigal journey. The book tells me about the Prodigal Son's journey away from home, it tells me about the blessings and gifts he's left behind, it tells me of all the downsides of the marketplace he left home for, but somehow the potential for a modern-day homecoming, while touched on, seems less clear, less proportionate to the other phases of the journey in the book. I wonder therefore whether there's another chapter on the Prodigal's return that makes the invisible hosting and hospitality of returners and the outgrowth of community and commons in neighborhoods across the world visible. I should say I know that that is done throughout the book, so this point may not be relevant; this exercise is highly subjective, but I found myself reading the book and throughout wondering where the Prodigal Son was going to appear.

WARD MAILLIARD

This is a quest to rediscover liturgy of the neighborhood.

Whales singing
   across the deep.
      We mortals feel the longing,
               sweet sadness
       of leviathan shapes
        in liquid ballet
         twining,
            calling to other.
  We land animals
      must now learn to bow
      to something
        more ancient.

The book delves into the alternate possibilities, and begins to develop language for a new conversation. It touches on the areas that matter in daily life. It addresses the misdirection of consumerism and provides a map for the wilderness. Both prose and poetry.

A few points to cheer about:

"Trust is the glue of the communal narrative."

"The point is to overcome our isolation."

"The collectiveness has been taken out of the spiritual experience."

"Community is the reconstruction of individual well-being through the well-being of the whole." and the rest of that paragraph !!!!

Question: "What to do with a broken story?"

"The act of imagination is to believe in the wilderness."

"The right use of wealth is an emotional and spiritual question."

"Mobility and isolation work hand in hand in the empire narrative."

"Commodity replaces narrative."

"Totalitarian regimes always have to call things by their wrong name."

"So the path is always an alternative to the track that is laid down by the dominant narrative."

"When the commons evaporate, so does the culture."

"Observance of the Sabbath is also a struggle against the market empire."

"The argument against the neighborly way is that we don't have time for that."

"Freedom in faithfulness."

"Every local place has to create a unique thing, something that cannot be taken to scale."

I think anyone and everyone who has "gone over the wall" or contemplated leaving the land of Pharaoh [will find the book useful]. You are mapping the wilderness. The intuitive yearning of sensing that we need to do some things differently is present in so many. I meet young people all the time who intuitively know that they need to find alternatives, but there is no effective description of what that means, or how it pertains to the specifics of an actual life. Hence, the attempt to live in the wilderness is short lived before re-absorption.

Final musing,
We always have a chance to end empire.
         What holds us back?

   The inducements of Pharaoh without,
            and alas, the pharaoh within,
                  continually canonizing comfort, security, the known way.

   On this tri-partate altar we sacrifice
            health, joy, family, sacredness, mystery,
                        and even this precious moment.

   Busy is our virus of choice,
            an excuse .... safe.
   The hungry ghost consumes,
            never satisfied and fearful,
                  Pharaoh is reborn.

DAVID CAYLEY

Writer and broadcaster, retired after forty years with CBC Radio, whose books include *The Rivers North of the Future: The Testament of Ivan Illich*.

I think some of the terms and concepts need to be more fully developed. I see that the book's purpose is, broadly speaking, prophetic rather than analytic, but even so I think it would be good to put more flesh on terms like "the commons." What were commons? I think that Lewis Hyde in his *Common as Air* does a good job in showing the complexity of the regime that governed common lands before their enclosure. It's hard to imagine the reinstitution of such a regime. So what does it mean concretely to imagine a restoration of commons.

[One of my recent] essay[s] begins with the story of Antonio Nebrija (1441–1522), a Spanish scholar who, in 1492, approached Queen Isabella of Spain in the hope of winning her support for his plan to write a formal grammar of the Castilian language. In that way he told her the untutored and unruly speech of her subjects could be brought under control and a new instrument of government created for the overseas dominions she was about to acquire. "Language," he says, "has always been the consort of empire." Nebrija anticipated great things from Columbus's voyage to the West, then still in progress, but he tried to persuade the queen that his grammar might be an even more auspicious undertaking. Spain would acquire a language comparable to the languages of antiquity, and the wild speech of her peoples would be brought under domestic cultivation.

Illich, shockingly, treats this quite differently. He sees Nebrija's grammar as the draft of "a declaration of war against subsistence," by which Illich means roughly things that people can do for themselves, like their ability to speak, acquire livelihood, live, and die outside of formal institutions. What glimmers at the horizon for Illich is not the flowering of national literatures but Orwell's Newspeak, the possibility of a totally administered language.

The vernacular, for Illich, is a figure of spontaneity, referring, by definition, to a domain that can neither be economized nor brought under professional management and manipulation. Such domains have only a fugitive existence in the contemporary world, and Illich was no more successful in establishing the concept than he was in rehabilitating gender. What he was seeking, as I now see it, was a science of complementarity—a view of things in which everything exists by reason of and in relation to its opposite. However, I don't think this is always clear in Illich's writing because it is sometimes obscured by a satirical and anti-modernist spirit that can make his critique seem more total than, at his best, he wants it to be.

DOUGLAS LARSEN SELL

ELCA [Evangelical Lutheran Church in America] pastor, Spring Green, Wisconsin

Perhaps the title might be "Who Is My Neighbor?" The question that Jesus responds with the parable of the Good Samaritan. That parable is to me a theme of the last third of the book.

The working title reminds me of Luther's idea of God's Two Kingdoms. And of Niebuhr's Christ and Culture. . . is Christ above, in, or under culture?

MICHAEL COFFEY

Rev. Michael Coffey, pastor of First English Lutheran Church (ELCA), Austin, Texas; author of *Mystery Without Rhyme or Reason: Poetic Reflections on the Revised Common Lectionary,* Wipf & Stock, Publishers. Blogger at www .ocotillopub.org.

The book's attempt to dismantle the hold on our imaginations that the market economy has is important and central. The contrast between contract and covenant is helpful. The hopeful exploration of what neighborly life looks like once reimagined is what I value and would hope to hear more of.

I would love to hear more exploration of the economic themes of the book in conversation with some of the current economists who are making similar critiques of the market ideology. Paul Krugman, Joseph Stiglitz, and even Thomas Piketty could be helpful conversation partners in offering both a critique of the current ideology and practical suggestions for alternative ways to imagine the economy for the sake of the common good.

I think for anyone who is under forty, it could be valuable to suggest how technology can be used for its own subversion, which is often what young people are using it for.

This book is for pastors, thoughtful lay people, those outside the church who might find this alternative vision of faith and faithful living an appealing inroads to exploring faith and scripture.

WALTER T. DAVIS, JR.

Professor of the Sociology of Religion (emeritus), San Francisco Theological Seminary, whose recent publications include *Zionism Unsettled: A Congregational Study Guide* and *Zionism and the Quest for Justice in the Holy Land*, co-edited with Donald E. Wagner.

The whole book is a *tour de force*. You asked us to "quickly read." I tried this, and my first impression was too much repetition of the same ideas. Then I realized that this book requires slow, meditative, reflective reading. So, I slowed down and began to see the interrelatedness of the ideas in a new light, how each repetition develops a different nuance and deepens the analysis of a particular aspect of the free market consumer culture.

Now I see the book as a spiral like a descending ladder: "every round goes deeper, deeper. . . ." Maybe what you have created resembles a symphony wherein one theme is repeated again and again, but each time interwoven with new themes.

I am struck by the style. You took the gloves off. No hedging or qualifying, just straight talk challenging the Golden Calf. Rarely have I read so much in so few words.

The personal comments gave the text a more intimate tone, as did the many examples of neighborly covenants. The sections on mystery and the place for God open up for me reflections about fundamental-ism in both science and religion.

I wonder if you might add a paragraph or two on how the free market consumer ideology requires a totalist military and foreign policy. This may be pushing the envelope a bit, but it is so central to the current system that its inclusion would strengthen your analysis (imho).

Preachers, local congregations, and denominational leaders with responsibilities in the areas of justice, peacemaking, and relief assis-tance [would consider this book useful].

ARTHUR LYONS

I wish I had been in on your conversations! I am fully in accord with what I understand to be your main point—that as a society we need a new imagination about priorities, including the non-material world and relationships that we now either don't see or we believe (without evidence) to be impossible. It's our entire culture that's at stake, and it needs to change. Reformative actions will flow from new ways of thinking.

Among the many specific ideas I like are the way you develop the notion of *kairos*. . . . The good ending will come if we each keep doing our part; we never know what the precipitating event will be. In a word, hope. Your concluding statement from the *Marigold Hotel* movie is a perfect tie-up.

I like how you clarify the costs, or the things we lose, because of our belief in the free market consumer ideology, for example, your section "Convenience Displaces Capacity." Like any culture, the free market ideology comes with blinders that allow us to see only the culture's real or presumed benefits, not its costs. Someone with experience outside the culture (in this case, you) is needed to make the costs visible.

I work with some groups trying to keep alcohol and other drugs away from teenagers, mostly high school students. Some of the youth say things like: Why not get stoned? Our parents all want us not only to get into college, but go to the best schools. We can't all go to the best schools. It's impossible. Why try?

These teens, their parents, and the school personnel who are afflicted with the "highest-grades" and "best-school" mentality are my first candidates for people who would find the book useful, if we could open their eyes to understand it.

I also do work on tax policy. Nearly everyone I meet—from government officials who collect and spend tax money to individuals who pay taxes—explicitly believes that it is a citizen's duty to take advantage of every possible loophole in the tax code and to pay the smallest amount of tax possible. Virtually no one begins with a sense of community or the realization that we are in sociopolitical relationships with each other, and taxes support *our* community.

I see this as one particular manifestation of the harmful individualism you discuss. As a society, we could have much more reasonable conversations about tax and spending policies—and an actually reasonable tax code—if either (a) enough policy-makers read and understood your book or (b) enough citizen-voters read and understood your book to impose a more rational discourse on politicians. (In my judgment, (b) is more likely to succeed.)

MARK ANIELSKI

Happiness economist and author of *The Economics of Happiness: Building Genuine Wealth.*

The book nails down that the current system is a shift from a covenant people living in relative "harmony" on the common "wealth" to one of contract law founded on an economic ideology of individualism, individual property rights, greed, hedonism, and utility maximization (more stuff is better). You don't try to identify the source of this ideology. I would argue that it was amplified by the work of Ayn Rand, who influenced the twentieth century economists, including Milton Friedman and Allan Greenspan; that society is "dead" and altruism is not a human characteristic.

You remind us of the wisdom that First Nations (Native Americans) still retain today: the truth of abundance as found in nature. It is no wonder we domination nations wanted to suppress celebrations of abundance like the potlatch! The potlatch was a mimic of nature in how nature gave without expectation and in rich abundant flourishing.

Nature gives without expectations of any return including our thank you. This is how the coastal First Nations lived. It was honorable to give from one's bounty to the rest of the community. This was followed by the next family who hosted the potlatch. The Israelites did not have such a practice. While God showed Moses and the Israelites to trust His mercy and abundance (Manna from the sky) they were very stubborn and wanted to return to the slavery and good eats of Egypt rather than die in the desert. First Nations never had that experience and somehow had wisdom that no other nation or place on earth seemed to have experienced.

The book will hopefully lift many hearts and minds with hope that indeed "home and neighborhood is where the heart is; where find community, joy and, most importantly, the truth of abundance."

It could spark a new conversation of the joy of neighborliness and relationships. When people learn again the truth of abundance and the joy of giving and receiving, the dark era of the slavery of greed and materialism will be over. The Wizard of Oz(s) will be unveiled for who they are; timid men with no joy in their hearts.

REFERENCES AND FURTHER READING

Below are the works we mention in text, those from which we have quoted directly, and sources from which we learned facts not commonly known. We have also listed those that have helped us to form our ideas, as well as a couple of our own previous books. At the end of the list, we have included some of the websites we contribute to, plus some we follow or which follow our work. If we have unknowingly extracted, in good colonial fashion, any ideas from you, please let us know and we will make amends and give full credit when the opportunity arises.

Alexander, Christopher, Ishikawa, Sara, and Silverstein, Murray. *A Pattern Language: Towns, Buildings, Construction.* New York: Oxford University Press, 1977.

Anielski, Mark. *The Economics of Happiness: Building Genuine Wealth.* Gabriola Island, BC, Canada: New Society Publishers, 2007.

——————. Email to Peter Block, Walter Brueggemann, and John McKnight. August 14, 2015.

Arrien, Angeles. *The Four-Fold Way: Walking the Paths of the Warrior, Teacher, Healer, and Visionary.* San Francisco: HarperOne, 1993.

Barnes, Peter. *With Liberty and Dividends for All: How to Save Our Middle Class When Jobs Don't Pay Enough.* San Francisco: Berrett-Koehler, 2014.

Bell, Rob. *Love Wins: A Book About Heaven, Hell, and the Fate of Every Person Who Ever Lived.* New York: HarperOne, 2011.

Bellah, Robert N., Madsen, Richard, Sullivan, William M., Swidler, Ann, and Tipton, Steven M. *Habits of the Heart: Individualism and Commitment in American Life.* Rev. ed. Oakland, CA: University of California Press, 2007. Originally published 1985.

Bishop, Bill. *The Big Sort: Why the Clustering of Like-Minded America Is Tearing Us Apart.* New York: Mariner Books, 2009.

Block, Peter. *Community: The Structure of Belonging.* San Francisco: Berrett-Koehler, 2008.

Brown, Ellen Hodgson. *Web of Debt: The Shocking Truth About Our Money System and How We Can Break Free.* 5th ed. Baton Rouge, LA: Third Millennium Press, 2012.

Brueggemann, Walter. *Sabbath as Resistance: Saying No to the Culture of Now.* Louisville, KY: Westminster John Knox Press, 2014.

——————. *Journey to the Common Good.* Louisville, KY: Westminster John Knox Press, 2010.

——————. *The Message of the Psalms: A Theological Commentary.* Minneapolis, MN: Augsburg Press, 2004. Originally published 1983.

——————. *The Prophetic Imagination.* 2nd ed. Minneapolis, MN: Augsburg Fortress, 2001. Originally published 1978.

——————. *Theology of the Old Testament: Testimony, Dispute, Advocacy.* Minneapolis, MN: Augsburg Fortress, 1997.

Byrd, Robert C. *The Senate, 1789–1989: Classic Speeches, 1830–1993.* Washington, DC: Government Printing Office, 1994.

Cahn, Edgar S. *Time Dollars: The New Currency That Enables Americans to Turn Their Hidden Resource—Time—into Personal Security and Community Renewal.* Emmaus, PA: Rodale Press, 1992.

——————. *No More Throw-Away People: The Co-Production Imperative.* 2nd ed. Washington, DC: Essential Books, 2004. Originally published 2000.

Carson, Rachel. *The Silent Spring: The Classic That Launched the Environmental Movement.* Anniversary edition. New York: Houghton Mifflin, 2002. Originally published 1962.

Cayley, David. *The Rivers North of the Future: The Testament of Ivan Illich, as Told to David Cayley.* Toronto: House of Anansi Press, 2005.

——————. Email to John McKnight. August 13, 2015.

Dostoyevsky, Fyodor. *The Brothers Karamazov.* Paperback reissue. New York: Oxford University Press, 2008. Originally published 1880.

Ellul, Jacques. *The Meaning of the City.* Eugene, OR: Wipf and Stock, 2011. Originally published 1970.

Esteva, Gustavo, Babones, Salvatore, and Babcicky, Philipp. *The Future of Development: A Radical Manifesto.* Bristol, UK: Policy Press, 2013.

Fed Up. Atlas Films. 2014.

Fishbane, Michael. *Sacred Attunement: A Jewish Theology.* Chicago: University of Chicago Press, 2008.

Friedan, Betty. *The Feminine Mystique.* 50th Anniversary Edition. New York: W.W. Norton, 2013. Originally published 1963.

Golding, William. *Lord of the Flies.* New York: Penguin, 2013. Originally published 1959.

Haskins, Minnie Louise. "God Knows" [or, "The Gate of the Year"]. In *The Desert*. London: 1908.

Illich, Ivan. *Shadow Work*. London: Marion Boyars, 1981.

—————. *Tools for Conviviality*. London: Marion Boyars, 2001. Originally published 1973.

—————. *The Right to Useful Unemployment: And Its Professional Enemies*. London: Marion Boyars, 2000. Originally published 1978.

Kohn, Alfie. *No Contest: The Case Against Competition*. Rev. ed. Boston: Houghton-Mifflin, 1992.

Kretzmann, John P., and McKnight, John L. *Building Communities from the Inside Out: A Path Toward Finding and Mobilizing a Community's Assets*. Evanston, IL: The Asset-Based Community Development Institute, 1993. Distributed by ACTA Publications, Chicago.

Kundera, Milan. *The Unbearable Lightness of Being*. Twentieth Anniversary Edition. New York: Harper, 2004. Originally published 1984.

McKnight, John, and Block, Peter. *The Abundant Community: Awakening the Power of Families and Neighborhoods*. San Francisco: Berrett-Koehler, 2010.

McKnight, John. *The Careless Society: Community and Its Counterfeits*. New York: Basic Books, 1995.

Mishra. Pankaj. *From the Ruins of Empire: The Intellectuals Who Remade Asia*. New York: Farrar, Straus and Giroux, 2012.

Muller, Jerry Z. *The Mind and the Market: Capitalism in Western Thought*. New York: Anchor, 2003.

Paper, Lewis J. *Empire: William S. Paley and the Making of CBS*. New York, St. Martin's Press, 1987.

Putnam, Robert D. *Making Democracy Work: Civic Traditions in Modern Italy*. Princeton, NJ: Princeton University Press, 1993.

Reba Place Fellowship. www.rebaplacefellowship.org/Home

Restakis, John. *Humanizing the Economy: Co-operatives in the Age of Capital*. Gabriola Island, BC: New Society Publishers, 2010.

Roche, Bruno B., and Jakub, Jay F. "The Economics of Mutuality," *The Brewery Journal*, January 2014.

Sachs, Wolfgang (ed.) *The Development Dictionary: A Guide to Knowledge as Power*. 2nd ed. London: Zed Books, 2009.

Schumacher, E.F. *Small Is Beautiful: Economics as if People Mattered*. Reprint ed. New York: Harper Perennial, 2010. Originally published 1975.

Wills, Garry. *Lincoln at Gettysburg: The Words That Remade America*. New York: Simon & Schuster, 2006.

Yousuf, Hibah. "School gives 16-year-olds $100,000 to invest," June 13, 2013. http://money.cnn.com/2013/06/13/investing/high-school-investing-club/

Websites

The following websites are a window into the backstory of what is highlighted in the book.

1. Here are sites of thought leaders that will take you deeper into their thinking:

   http://aletmanski.com/

   http://robertdputnam.com/

   www.alfiekohn.org/

   www.davidcayley.com/

   www.anielski.com/

   www.walterbrueggemann.com

2. Here are a few leading organizations in the neighborliness movement:

   http://democracycollaborative.org/—One home for work of Gar Alparovitz

   http://timebanks.org/—A social invention of Edgar Cahn

   www.abcdinstitute.org—The community work of Jody Kretzmer and John McKnight. Where Asset Based Community Development was born.

   www.abundantcommunity.com—Documents what citizens are doing to create neighborliness.

   www.designedlearning.com—The workshops growing out of Peter's writings.

   www.highlandscommunity.ca/abundantcommunities.html.—More on the implementation of neighborhood work.

   www.restore-commons.com—An initial attempt at a collecting place for the ideas driving the other kingdom.

   www.sbs.ox.ac.uk/ideas-impact/research-projects/mutuality-business—The work Mars Inc and its partners are doing to re-imagine the purpose of a business.

   www.yesmagazine.org/—The storyteller of where an alternative culture is occurring.

www.Axiomnews.ca—Constructing a generative journalism and narrative art that builds community rather than feeding on its wounded-ness.

3. There is one group that warrants special mention. Susan Witt leads the Schumacher Center for a New Economics, the roots of which stretch back to E.F. Schumacher. Few groups have been as inventive and enduring in starting efforts to support the common good. They are the spiritual and educational Mecca for creating a world that cares for every citizen, every parcel of soil, and every community. Here are the websites, including their own, that have been inspired or been launched out of the work of this group.

   www.centerforneweconomics.org—The Mother ship.

   Berkshares.org—BerkShares Local Currency.

   Communitylandtrust.org—Community Land Trust in the Southern Berkshires.

   www.agroecologynetwork.org—Cuba U.S. Agroecology Network.

   Centerforneweconomics.org/college—Schumacher College for a New Economics.

   www.codepink.org/peaceeconomy—CodePink Local Peace Economy Campaign.

   www.berrycenter.org—The Berry Center.

   https://Bealocalist.org—BALLE.

   www.postcarbon.org—Post Carbon Institute.

   www.theSELC.org—Sustainable Economies Law Center.

   www.dsni.org—Dudley Street Neighborhood Initiative.

   https://islr.org—Institute for Local Self Reliance.

   welrp.org—White Earth Land Recovery Project.

   https://landinstitute.org—The Land Institute.

   rafiusa.org—Rural Advancement Foundation International.

   www.presencing.com—Presencing Institute.

ACKNOWLEDGMENTS

This book grew out several wide-ranging conversations over a year's time. It was not easy to be clear about the point of the book. The reader may still feel that way. Whatever clarity exists, it was greatly aided by some colleagues who read and commented on the manuscript along the way. Some of their response survives in the "Commentaries" section. But we want to thank them in one place for affection and friendship sent our way by their efforts.

Thanks to Bruce Anderson, Mark Anielski, David Cayley, Michael Coffey, Walt Davis, Al Etmanski, Kevin Jones, Larry (Robert) Inchausti, Howard Lawrence, Douglas Larson-Sell, Arthur Lyons, Ward Mailliard, and Cormac Russell.

There is also a team of people at Wiley who brought this book into being. Matt Holt, our publisher, took the big chance. He said he liked to publish a weird book every once in a while, so this was it. Liz Gildea has managed the production, listens carefully, and comes back with ideas completely in line with our intentions. Matt Davis, who came on as acquisition editor, is a colleague on another book and is always a joy. Dawn Kilgore has handled her phase of production with clarity and constant support. Thanks to copyeditor Rebecca Taff for her thoughtful touches. We also thank the cover and interior design team, including Michael Freeland, for their support.

Finally, Leslie Stephen is the developmental editor, which means she takes a set of rambling ideas and reconstructs them into what becomes a book. The content of the ideas always remains the fault of the authors, but if the book has any coherence and accessible structure, Leslie is the one who made that happen. And she does it with understanding and affection. Gracias.

ABOUT THE AUTHORS

This book is the convergence of three imaginations: a Prophetic/ Sacred Imagination, a Community Imagination, and a Workplace/ System Imagination. Imagination is fundamentally a shift in lens and language—whose voices we listen to, where we look to construct an alternative future. Each of us has, over too many years, cultivated different fields which came together in the conversations producing this book.

Here is a short and very cryptic list that hints at the paths that brought us together:

> *Walter:* Prophetic Imagination, Exodus, Lamentation, Contestation, Gratitude, Interruption, Un-credentialed King, Wilderness, Covenant, Crying Out, God, Covenant, Empire
>
> *John:* Community, Neighborliness, Association, Gifts, Hospitality, Friendship, Care, Service, Triangles and Circles, System
>
> *Peter:* Partnership, Consultation, Stewardship, Empowerment, Authenticity, Social Contract, Convening, Large and Small Group Structures, Conversations of Possibility and Ownership

PETER BLOCK

Peter Block was born in Chicago and spent most of his early years in the Midwest. After college, he went to New Jersey and was involved in the early days of creating the field of organization development. This entailed some years at Exxon Research and Engineering Company and then the formation of a consulting firm with Tony Petrella. Marvin Weisbord joined in 1971, and the firm played a part in many of the large change efforts of that era.

In 1980, Peter started Designed Learning, a training company that offers workshops based on the ideas in his books. It still thrives and works to help staff people in organizations to have more influence and impact.

In 1995, Peter became involved with city government and city managers through conferences held by the Innovations Group based in Florida. This led to his interest in building community, which has been his obsession ever since. Peter met John at a community conference convened by Police Chief Mike Butler in Longmont, Colorado. This is where their common view of the world became obvious to both of them, which eventually culminated in writing *The Abundant Community* together.

Peter has written seven other books, including *Flawless Consulting*, *The Empowered Manager*, *Stewardship*, *Freedom and Accountability* (with Peter Koestenbaum), *The Answer to How Is Yes*, and *Community: The Structure of Belonging*.

The community work is now centered in Cincinnati, Ohio, where Peter lives with his wife, Cathy Kramer. He is engaged in developing a civic engagement network called A Small Group, plus a series of other projects working on building the capacity of this urban community to value its gifts and see its own possibility. His most recent work there is with Walter Brueggemann and others in the Economics of Compassion Initiative of Greater Cincinnati, supporting alternative economic systems marked by justice, community, and relationship.

WALTER BRUEGGEMANN

Walter Brueggemann is one of the most influential Bible interpreters of our time. He is the author of more than one hundred books and numerous scholarly articles. He continues to be a highly sought-after speaker.

Walter was born in Tilden, Nebraska, in 1933. He often speaks of the influence of his father, a German Evangelical pastor. Walter attended Elmhurst College, graduating in 1955 with an A.B. He went on to Eden Theological Seminary, earning a B.D. (equivalent to today's M.Div.) in 1958. He completed his formal theological education at Union Theological Seminary in 1961, earning the Th.D. under the primary guidance of James Muilenburg. While teaching at Eden, he earned a Ph.D. in education at St. Louis University.

Walter has served as faculty at two institutions in his career: Eden Theological Seminary (1961–1986) and Columbia Theological Seminary (1986–2003). He is currently William Marcellus McPheeters professor emeritus of Old Testament at Columbia.

Walter's primary method with the sacred texts is rhetorical criticism. Words matter to Walter, and one can tell that by listening to him speak as he hangs on to particularly theologically significant words. His magnum opus, *Theology of the Old Testament*, is a rhetorical-critical look at the Old Testament through the lenses of "testimony, dispute, and advocacy."

Many have come to know Walter through his book entitled *The Prophetic Imagination*, originally published in 1978. His best-known work, however, may be with the Psalms. Numerous church leaders have used his *Message of the Psalms* as a new way of organizing and processing the Psalms. He has been writing about the Psalms since 1982, and he continues to this day with a commentary published in 2014.

Walter touches many of the themes in *An Other Kingdom* in *Journey to the Common Good,* in which he uses biblical texts to illuminate what is required to move from isolation and distrust to a practice of neighborliness.

Church leaders find a friend in Walter, an ordained minister in the United Church of Christ. His work inspires, energizes, and persuades, and he always makes time to interact personally with those to whom he speaks at large events.

Walter and his wife, Tia. currently reside in Cincinnati, Ohio, where he has been a driving force for the region's Economics of Compassion Initiative. He is a longtime St. Louis Cardinals/Browns fan.

JOHN L. MCKNIGHT

John L. McKnight was raised a traveling Ohioan, having lived in seven neighborhoods and small towns in the eighteen years before he left to attend Northwestern University, in Evanston, Illinois. There, he had the good fortune to be educated by a faculty dedicated to preparing students for effective citizenship. He graduated into the U.S. Navy, where he had three years of "postgraduate" education in Asia during the Korean War.

John returned to Chicago and began working for several activist organizations, including the Chicago Commission for Human Relations, the first municipal civil rights agency. There he learned the Alinsky trade called *community organizing*. This was followed by the directorship of the Illinois American Civil Liberties Union, where he organized local chapters throughout the state.

When John Kennedy was elected president, John was recruited into the federal government, where he worked with a new agency that created the affirmative action program. Later, he was appointed the Midwest director of the United States Commission on Civil Rights, where he worked with local civil rights and neighborhood organizations.

In 1969, John's alma mater, Northwestern University, invited him to return and help initiate a new department called the Center for Urban Affairs. This was a group of interdisciplinary faculty doing research designed to support urban change agents and progressive urban policy. John's appointment was an act of heroism on the part of the university, as it gave him a tenured professorship, though he had only a bachelor's degree.

While at the center and its successor, the Institute for Policy Research, John and a few of his colleagues focused their research on urban neighborhoods. The best-known result of this work was the formulation of an understanding of neighborhoods focused on the usefulness of local resources, capacities, and relationships. This work was documented in a guide co-authored with John P. Kretzmann titled *Building Communities from the Inside Out,* describing an approach to community building that became a major development strategy practiced in North and South America, Europe, Africa, Asia, and Australia. As an aside, it was during this time that John was one of the trainers of Barack Obama as he learned the skills of community organizing.

John is also the author of *The Careless Society: Community and Its Counterfeits,* a classic critique of professionalized social services and a celebration of communities' ability to heal themselves from within.

John began working with Peter in practical explorations of how communities become "villages" with the capacity to raise their children, which culminated in their 2010 book, *The Abundant Community*. John and Peter also currently collaborate on www.abundantcommunity.com, which reflects their latest thinking on community work and documents stories of community-building efforts around the world.

INDEX

A

Abundance: as generative of more abundance, 3; good farming as the practice of, 3; neighborly belief and meaning of, 9–10; reclaiming the common good with, 20; the right use of money and, 75–77

Achan, 23

Addition, 23

Adult baptism, 74

Affliction: Bread of Affliction, 17–18; often associated with fallibility, 17

Agri-business scarcity practice, 3

Alexander, Christopher, 10

Aliveness: grief as having an element of, 19; market ideology as the end of, 39–40; qualities of wholeness and, 10

Allen, Woody, 81

Amish community, 28

Anabaptists, 74–75

Anielski, Mark, 67, 81–82, 94–95

Arrien, Angeles, 50

Associations, 49

AT&T humanizing training, 36

Autonomy: kickback from market ideology as fueled by, 50; as organizing principle of free market culture, 1–2

Axiom News, 82

B

Bank of North Dakota, 48, 76

Baseball: baseball park marriages, 78; the Sunday baseball tradition, 51

Beatitudes (New Testament), 52

Bell, Rob, 11

Bellah, Robert, 50

Benchmarking practice, 31

Bergoglio, Cardinal Jorge, 72

BerkShares currency, 75–76

The Best Exotic Marigold Hotel (*Marigold Hotel* film), 80, 93

Big-church growth movement, 58

The Big Sort (Bishop), 58–59

Bishop, Bill, 58–59

Block, Peter, 22

The blue laws debate, 51

Borsodi, Ralph, 76

Bread of Affliction, 17–18

British oppression. *See* Scotland

Broadway Ministry (Philadelphia), 65

"Broken person" (Scottish outcast), 30

Brown, Ellen Hodgson, 76

Brueggemann, Walter: attendance at conference about justice, 83; on being married in a ballpark, 78; on friend's food stamp rant, 35; working on program documenting movement toward exclusive communities, 58–59

Buffet, Warren, 23

Byrd, Robert C., 83

C

Cahn, Edgar, 54

Cain, 30

Capacity: the Amish's conscious approach to technology and its, 28; digital solutions to increase, 28–29; how convenience has displaced our, 27–28

Carnegie, Andrew, 23

Carson, Rachel, 83

Catholic Church: the contemplative orders of the, 72; seven sacraments of the, 80

Cayley, David, 10, 24, 50, 90–91

Certainty: as pillar of free market consumer ideology, 1, 2, 3; seeking predictability and safety through, 3

Chan, Edgar, 81

Change management, 31

Charity: co-production that replaces, 81; market culture mentality of, 39

Children: isolated from the adults in a community, 42–43; violent effects of mistrust of authority by, 43

The Church: Anabaptists' belief in adult baptism, 74–75; big-church growth movement of, 58; the Catholic Church contemplative orders, 72; the Eucharist of, 68, 79; Kairos Document of South African Churches against Apartheid, 66; Last Supper tradition of, 67–68; liturgy tradition of, 77, 79–80; Presbyterian churches celebrating their Scottish roots, 51; problem with the "You are friends" statement by Jesus, 79; seven sacraments of the Catholic Church, 80

Churchill, Winston, 12

Civil Rights Act (1964), 83

Civil Rights Movement, 82

Class warfare: corporate interest in staying blind to the inequalities of, 38–39; the cost of competition and underclass and, 33–34; the distribution of wealth driving, 34–35; schools as having moved to the frontline of the, 38; violence as consequences of the empire and, 42–43

Cleveland Foundation, 54

Coffey, Michael, 91–92

Commodification: embodied in food, 70; fast food and supermarket, 69, 70; loss of the commons and creating relationships of, 50

Common good: the desire for more leads to violation of, 23; how abundance, mystery, fallibility, and grief help us reclaim the, 20; a liturgy for the, 77–80; privatization as overthrowing the, 1, 2, 4

The commons: as alternative to the dominant market economy and reconstructing purpose, 48–49; the ideology of individualism conflicting with, 48; loss of memory in, 50; market ideology as breakdown the culture and, 49–50; Mennonites' Reba Place Fellowship example of, 52–53; Neighborly Covenant as central to community, 46–47

Community: aliveness of, 10–11; the Amish, 28; as constantly developing their own practices creating a memory of place, 80; covenantal or distributive justice and distribution of wealth of the, 75; documenting movement toward exclusive, 58–59; holiness associated with building, 15; how vernacular language sustains the covenant and keeps together a, 25, 50, 90–91; liturgy and spirituality of a communal and neighborly, 54–55; Mennonites' Reba Place Fellowship, 52–53; mysteries within culture and spiritual life of every, 12–13; neighborliness as welcoming strangers into the, 49; Neighborly Covenant as central to the commons and, 46–47; the shadow side of, 58–59; spirit and meaning of the Cuernavaca community market, 52; technology used to connect neighbors and, 28–29; tracing over time the benefits of institutions to the, 37; un-welcomingness of small, 58; urbanization and the loss of, 30–31

Community Connections group (Cleveland), 54

Competition: class warfare and the distribution of wealth, 34–35; consequences of school-driven, 32–33; free market belief in, 32–33; how cooperative activities beat, 32; scarcity constructing an economy of controlled quantities and, 2; as trumping trust, 5–6

Conboy, Edd, 65

"Constant" currency initiative (1972), 76

Consumer market: believing in a consumption-driven economy and, 31–32; believing in safety through economic growth of the, 31–32; class warfare driven by the, 33–35, 38–39; disciplines of the, 24–35; as the end of aliveness, 39–40; loss of the local and communal memory in a, 50; mobility and isolation outcomes of the, 40–41; un-productive wealth of the, 41–42; violence expression of the, 42–43. *See also* Contract culture; Free market consumer ideology

Consumer market disciplines: competition and class, 32–35; digital solutions, 28–29; the meaning of money, 29–32; predictability and control, 24–29; speed and convenience, 26–28, 63–65; surplus, 22–24

Contract culture: certainty and perfection value of, 1, 2, 3; free market as core conviction of the, 2; idea of needs, 1; indifference to gifts and focus on autonomy by, 1–2, 50; institutional assumptions of the, 4–6; memo commination of the, 18; organized around systems, 2; privatization value of, 1, 2, 3–4; scarcity value of the, 1, 2–3, 36, 42–44. *See also* Consumer market; Culture; Free market consumer ideology

Control: consumer market need for predictability and, 24–25; wishing for safety and believing in growth and, 31–32

Convenience: consumer ideology on relationship of speed and, 26; how it displaces capacity, 27–28; neighborly discipline of time in place of speed and, 63–65; technological support of speed and, 26–27

Co-operative food movement, 69

Cooperative movement: as alternative to productivity, 55–57; the power of the, 32

Corporations: the corporation of schools supporting, 38; illusion of reforms by, 43–44; interest in staying blind to social and economic inequality, 38–39

Covenant: Cain's break with God's, 30; as the expression of mystery, 10; God stands as someone who would make a, 74; how vernacular language keeps a community together and sustains, 25; Judaism *Shema* ("Hear") to be a listening people and faithful to the, 71–72; the neighborly culture as based on relatedness and, 6–7; retributive justice and, 75; to see the gifts of the widow and orphan, 57; traditionally with God or a high power, 62; as a vow of freedom and faithfulness, 74–75; wilderness as the Old Testament metaphor for social order of the, 15–16. *See also* Neighborly Covenant

Crime-making justice systems, 37

Culture: customs celebrating the resistance against the mother, 51; description and function of, 50; how food expresses a, 69–71; as manifesting a way of being, 55; market ideology as breakdown the commons and, 49–50; the shadow side of, 58–59; vernacular language importance to, 25, 50, 90–91. *See also* Contract culture

Currency: BerkShares, 75–76; "Constant," 76; counterfeiting of Federal, 76. *See also* Money

Cynicism about future, 21

D

Davis, Walter T., Jr., 92–93

Death-defying wealthy man, 14–15

Debt: belief in a consumption-driven economy and, 31–32; Deuteronomy 15 on Jubilee Year release from, 35, 65

Denial, 19

Developmentally disabled people movement, 17

Día de los Muertos, 51

Diet industry fraud, 70–71

Dirksen, Everett, 83

Distributive justice, 75

Domino's Pizza, 66

Dostoyevsky, Fyodor, 14

Dow Jones Industrial Average, 24, 54

E

The Economics of Happiness (Anielski), 81–82, 94

Ellul, Jacques, 30

The empire: the co-operative movement as alternative to, 48–49; forsaking the vernacular language for the language of the, 25, 50, 90–91; illusion of reform in the context of, 43–44; market control through the language of, 24, 25; resisting the, 50–51; schools as the center of the strength of, 38; violence as expression of the market culture and, 42–43

Enclosure: the commons as stance for life and reversing, 48, 90; driving the Scots off the land to be replaced with sheep, 45–46; fear as driving us to gather in tribal, 58; how it drove people off the land and toward urbanization, 30–31; as violation of community by the British, 4

Environmental Movement, 82

Episcopal House of Bishops, 58–59

The Eucharist, 68, 79

F

Faithfulness and freedom covenant, 74–75

Fallibility: failing to be God, 18–19; grief due to reality of, 19–20; neighborliness based on the knowledge of, 16–18; parallels between mystery and, 18; reclaiming the common good with, 20

Family dinner ritual, 68

Fast food commodification, 69, 70

Feast of San Gennaro, 51

Fed Up (documentary), 70–71

Federal Reserve, 76

The Feminine Mystique (Friedan), 82–83

Food: Christian Last Supper tradition of, 67–68; the co-operative food movement, 69; culture expressed through, 69–71; Jewish Passover Seder tradition of, 67; ritual of the family dinner and soul food made by mother, 68; sacred occasion of sharing and consuming, 66–67; as sacred re-performance, 67–68; social order signpost of, 62

Food and Drug Administration (FDA), 71

Food stamps rant, 35

Free market consumer ideology: consumer market disciplines of the, 22–35; as the end of aliveness, 39–40; fast food and supermarket process food as foundational to, 69; the four pillars of the, 1, 2–4; free market as core conviction of the, 2; institutional assumptions of the, 4–6; memo communication of the, 18; monopoly as the unstated intention of, 1; the myth of individualism in, 36; neighborliness as alternative social order to, 49–50; reliance on the idea of needs satisfied by buying and selling, 1; the shrinking middle class as one consequence of the, 21; on the "underserving" vulnerable, 39. *See also* Consumer market; Contract culture

Free market consumer ideology pillars: certainty, 1, 2, 3, 12; perfection, 1, 2, 3; privatization, 1, 2, 3–4; scarcity, 1, 2–3

Freedom and faithfulness covenant, 74–75

Friedan, Betty, 82

Friendship. *See* Personal relationships

G

Gang violence, 42–43

Gay Rights Movement, 83

Generosity: the economy of a non-monetized, 30; how monopoly and scarcity creates a context without, 36; TimeBanking developing a measure for, 81

Genuine Well-Being Index, 81

George VI, King, 12

Gettysburg Address, 48

Gifts: contract culture vs. neighborly culture focus on, 1–2, 50; covenant to see the vulnerable and their, 57; Mennonites' Reba Place Fellowship and their teachables, 53

God: belief that kings and right to rule were commissioned by, 48; Cain's broken covenant with, 30; failing to be, 18–19; Hebrew Bible's presentation as a mystery who comes with a narrative, 13; neighborly covenant and mystery providing a place for, 13–15; risk of public or civic space conversations about, 14; as someone who would make a Covenant, 74; Tree of Knowledge on the Holy Mystery of, 14

Golding, William, 43

Good questions, 73–74

Gregorian calendar, 64

Gregory XIII, Pope, 64

Grief: as element of fallibility, 19; reclaiming the common good with, 20

Gross Domestic Product, 54, 81

H

"Habits of the heart," 50

Hallet, Stan, 27

Hand of God speech (King George VI), 12

Haskins, Minnie Louise, 12

Hezekiah, King, 24

Holiday Inn, 12

Holiness, 15

Hopi Indians (Black Mesa area), 79

Huzekiah, King, 24

I

Illich, Ivan: on Antonio Nebrija's Castilian language request, 24–25, 90, 91; on institutions as being counter-productive, 37; *The Right to Useful Unemployment* by, 57; *Shadow Work* by, 24; *Tools for Conviviality* by, 10; on transforming experience of grief, 19; on "vernacular" social life, 50

Illusion of reform, 43–44

Inchausti, Robert, 85–86

Individualism: the commons as conflicting with the ideology of, 48; contrasting between Sweden's commons approach and U.S., 48; the myth of, 36

Infant baptism, 74

Institutional assumptions: better management/ technology is the fix, 4–5; competition trumps trust, 5–6; interpersonal is a problem, 5

Institutions: assumptions of the, 4–6; Ivan Illich on tracing the community benefits received from, 37; as structure of preference by the contract culture, 2

Isabella (queen of Spain), 24–25, 90

Isai, 24

Isaiah, 24

Israelites: Bread of Affliction (bread of Pharaoh), 17–18; Judaism *Shema* ("Hear") to be a listening people, 71–72; in the wilderness, 15–16; wishing for safety while in the wilderness, 31, 81. *See also* Old Testament

J

Jesus: healing lepers, 3; introducing the Last Supper to his disciples, 78–79; the problem the Church has had with the "You are friends" statement of, 79

Joshua, 23

Jubilee Year, 35, 65

Junior Achievement program, 29

Justice: as beginning with a vow to freedom and fidelity, 12; covenantal or distributive, 75; Covenant and retributive, 75; relationship between mystery and, 12; young Evangelical Christians attending a conference about, 83

K

Kairos, 65–66, 93

Kairos Document (South African Churches), 66

King, Martin Luther, Jr., 11

"Kitsch" religion, 19

Kohn, Alfie, 32

Kundera, Milan, 19

L

Language: cultural importance of vernacular, 25, 50, 90–91; English attempt to stamp out Gaelic to control Scotland, 50–51; market control through the language of empire, 24, 25; Mother Tongue, 25, 50; Nebrija's request to Queen Isabella on the Castilian, 24–25, 90; predictability and control through Business Perspective, 24, 25–26

Last Supper tradition, 67–68

Law of Release, 35

Lawrence, Howard, 82

Lenin, Vladimir, 83

Leprosy healing stories, 3

Lincoln, Abraham, 48

Lincoln at Gettysburg: Words That Remade America (Wills), 48

Listening: Judaism *Shema* ("Hear") call to, 71–72; the Quakers' use of time and, 72–73; understanding the value of, 72

Liturgy: the Church tradition of, 77, 79–80; for the common good, 77–80; description of, 77; holding the prophecy over time, 78–79; the re-performance power of, 79–80; story as re-performance and, 79

Lord of the Flies (Golding), 43

Love, 3

Love Wins (Bell), 11

Luddites, 26

Lyons, Arthur, 93–94

M

McKnight, John: on developmentally disabled son mediating father to God, 17; on grieving what you cannot change, 19; on *No Contest: The Case Against Competition* on power of cooperation, 32; "On the Incredible Possibilities of Failing to Be God" hypothetical essay title by, 18; spirit and meaning of the Cuernavaca community market, 52; State Street Theater sit-in (1949) participation by, 82

Mailliard, Ward, 88–89

Management: change, 31; institutional belief in solutions through better, 4–5; the Mother Tongue in the language of, 25, 50

Mardi Gras, 51

Marigold Hotel (film), 80, 93

Market ideology. *See* Free market consumer ideology

Massachusetts Bay Colony, 48

Mayan foodway, 69

The Meaning of the City (Ellul), 30

Meaningful life, 10

Mechanization, 30

Mediterranean diet, 69–70, 71

Memo communication, 18

Memory: the common as loss of, 50; community practices that create a place of, 80; consumer market as loss of local and communal, 50; as a narrative in a place generating prophecy, 78; story as liturgy and re-performance, 79

Mennonites' Reba Place Fellowship, 52–53

Mobility: consumer market outcome of, 40–41; as modern vehicle for encouraging exclusive communities, 59

Money: abundance and the right use of, 75–77; examining the meaning of, 29–32; how love of profit corrupts, 23–24; Junior Achievement program's purpose to teach students about, 29; making money on, 23; mechanization and urbanization of, 30–31; our affection for place and, 77; student loans crisis, 76–77; time as, 64. *See also* Currency; Wealth

Monopoly: creating a context without generosity, 36; as free market consumer intention, 1

Mother Tongue language, 25, 50

Muste, Reverend A. J., 73

Mystery: as creating a space for surprise, 12–13; as embodiment of spiritual life, 10, 13; holiness, 15; how technology has eradicated, 27; as opening the door to a neighborhood organized by covenant, 10; parallels between fallibility and, 18; providing a place for God, 13–15; reclaiming the common good with, 20; relationship between justice and, 12;

silence as a companion of listening and, 71–73; wilderness, 15–16; the work of, 11–13

The myth of individualism, 36

N

National People's Action, 55

Navajo tribe, 79

Nebrija, Antonio, 24–25, 90

Neighborhood: customs celebrating the resistance against the mother culture and keeping alive the, 51; the modern disappearance of the, 7; technology used to connect community and, 28–29

Neighborliness: as alternative social order to market ideology, 49–50; a cooperative movement constructing practices of, 56–57; the disciplines of, 61–74; found in the Old Testament wilderness, 49, 57; liturgy for the common good and, 77–80; moving toward, 7; off-modern possibilities of, 51–53; welcoming strangers into the community, 49. *See also* Personal relationships

Neighborliness disciplines: food as a, 62, 66–71; introduction to the, 61–63; silence as a, 62, 71–74; time as a, 62, 63–66

Neighborly beliefs: abundance, 3, 9–10, 20, 75–77; the common good, 1, 2, 4, 20, 23, 77–80; fallibility, 16–20; mystery, 10–18, 20, 71–73

Neighborly Covenant: as central to the commons and community, 46–47; description and implications of, 62; neighborly beliefs of the, 9–20; supporting neighborly disciplines, 6–7. *See also* Covenant

Neighborly culture: based on covenant and relatedness, 6–7; benefits of moving toward a, 6; focus on possessions as having been a gift, 1–2; liturgy and spirituality of a communal, 54–55; privatization as overthrowing the common good and, 1, 2, 4

New Testament: the Beatitudes of the, 52; Ecclesiastes on time for all seasons idea, 64; *Kairos* concept in the, 66, 93; off-market Moses movement in the, 52

New Testament
  Matthew
    24:36, **71**
    25, **34**
  Luke
    7:44–46, **37**
    10:36, **53**
    12:18, **1**
    18:23, **29**
  Acts 20:35, **61**
  Romans, 12:13, **67**
  I Corinthians, 13:1–2, **2**
  See also Old Testament
Nextdoor.com, 28
Nimrod (the first city), 30
No Contest: The Case Against Competition
  (Kohn), 32
Northern vs. southern Italian economy, 49

O
Obesity, 71
O'Brien, Tom, 54
Off-modern possibilities, 51–53
Old Testament: on Jubilee Year release from
    debt, 35, 65; neighborliness found in
    the wilderness of, 49, 57; off-market
    Moses movement in the, 52; Ten
    Commandments of the, 15, 23, 52; Tree
    of Knowledge in the, 14; wilderness as the
    metaphor for social order of the covenant
    in, 15–16. *See also* Israelites
Old Testament
  Leviticus 19:18, **6**
  Deuteronomy
    8, **14–15**
    15, **35**
    15:7, **32**
    23:3, **3**
  Psalms
    31:15, **65**
    146, **34**
  Proverbs 25:2, **10**
  Isaiah
    47:8, **21**
    56:7, **45**
    61, **34**
  Jeremiah 8:7, **55**
  See also New Testament

Outsiders: Scottish "broken person" outcast
    or, 30; un-welcoming-ness of small
    community to, 58

P
Paley, William, 18
Paper, Lewis J., 18
Parochialism, 58
Passover Seder, 67Paul, Apostle, 1, 18
Pax Britannica, 58
Perfection: "failure is not an option" belief of, 3;
    as pillar of free market consumer ideology,
    1, 2, 3
Personal relationships: assumed to be an
    institutional "problem," 5; loss of the
    commons and loss of un-commodified
    friendship and, 50; neighborly culture
    based on covenant and, 6–7. *See also*
    Neighborliness
Pharaoh's reach: Israelites going into the
    wilderness to be beyond, 15–16; modern
    analog of being, 16
Place: community practices that create a memory
    of, 80; of local economy and businesses, 77
Poverty: anger against food stamps and those
    "poor people" in, 35; duty to protect the
    vulnerable and those in, 34–35; market
    ideology on the "undeserving" state of, 39;
    the meaning and implications of, 30. *See
    also* Wealth
Predictability: believing in growth and wishing for
    safety and, 31–32; consumer market need
    for control and, 24–25; how language
    supports control and, 24–25. *See also*
    Uncertainty
Privatization: the co-operative movement as
    alternative to, 48–49; as overthrowing the
    common good, 4; as pillar of free market
    consumer ideology, 1, 2, 4
Productivity: abundance of gifts related to, 53;
    cooperative movement as the alternative
    to, 55–57; Ivan Illich on institutions as
    being counter-productivity, 37; to listen as
    a retreat from, 72; observance of Sabbath
    as protest against, 51
Prophecy: liturgy as holding prophecy over time,
    78–79; memory as a narrative in a place
    generates, 78

Pula, Peter, 82
Putnam, Robert D., 49

Q

The Quakers, 72–73
"Quality of aliveness," 10
Questions and silence, 73–74

R

Reba Place Fellowship, 52–53
Reform: as illusion in the context of empire and
     scarcity, 43–44; transformation required
     for genuine, 44
Relationships. *See* Personal relationships
Religion: "kitsch" (religion that doesn't tell all
     the truth), 19; mandra on spirituality
     without, 14
Re-performance: food as sacred, 67–68; power of
     liturgy as, 79–80; story as liturgy and, 79
Retributive justice, 75
The Right to Useful Unemployment (Illich), 57
Risk management, 12
Rotary Clubs, 24
Russell, Cormac, 86–87

S

Sabbath: to listen as a form of, 72; observance of
     the, 51
Sacraments of silence, 73–74
Scarcity: agri-business as practice of, 3;
     constructing economy of controlled
     quantities and competition, 2; creating a
     context without generosity, 36; illusion of
     reform in the context of, 43–44; as pillar
     of free market consumer ideology, 1, 2–3;
     violence as expression of class distinctions
     and, 42–43
School-driven competition, 32–33
Schools: class warfare driving by the corporation
     of, 38; consequences of the competition
     driven by, 32–33; illusion of reform of, 43
Schumacher, E. E., 28
Scotland: "broken person" outcast in, 30;
     enclosure driving the Scots off the land to
     be replaced with sheep, 45–46; English
     attempt to stamp out Gaelic to control,

50–51; Presbyterian churches celebrating
     their Scottish roots, 51
Second World War, 12
Seel, Douglas Larsen, 91
Shadow Work (Illich), 24
Shema ("Hear"), 71–72
Sickness-making medical systems, 37
Silence: as a companion of mystery and listening,
     71–73; sacraments of, 73–74; social order
     signpost of, 62
The Silent Spring (Carson), 83
Small Is Beautiful (Schumacher), 28
Social change movements: examples of triggers for
     historic, 82–83; signs of change driving,
     83
Soul food of home, 68
Southern vs. northern Italian economy, 49
Speed: consumer market disciplines of
     convenience and, 26–28; neighborly
     discipline of time in place of modern,
     63–65
Spirituality: mantra on spirituality without
     religion, 14; mystery as embodiment of a
     life of, 10, 13
Standing in line time, 65
State Street Theater sit-in (1949), 82
Stonewall riots (Greenwich Village), 83
Story: community built on the power of, 79;
     the eleven creation stories of the Hope
     Indians, 79; as liturgy and re-performance,
     79; wealthy man who hates death, 14–15
Student loans, 76–77
Sunday baseball tradition, 51
Sunday closing laws, 51
Super Bowl mentality, 78
Supermarket commodification, 69, 70
Surplus: consumer market, 22–24; we have come
     to identify ourselves by our privilege
     and, 22
Swedish communal-minded culture, 48

T

Technology: the Amish's conscious approach
     to, 28; expanding its influence into
     community space and capacity, 28–29;
     institutional belief in solutions through,
     4–5; luddite argument against, 26; speed
     and convenience as selling points of,

26–27; un-measured burden as the hidden cost of, 27

Ten Commandments: Moses movement and the, 52; the Tenth Commandment of the, 15, 23

Time: for all things, 63; anti-system nature of, 63–64; Ecclesiastes on time for all seasons idea of, 64; how the Quakers use listening and, 72–73; modern social construction of, 64; money as, 64; social order signpost of, 62; standing in line, 65

TimeBanking, 81

Tools for Conviviality (Illich), 10

Torah: collision between our free market narrative and the, 35; on obligation of the community to protect the vulnerable, 34; the way of the, 10

Trappist monks, 72

Tree of Knowledge, 14

Trust, 5–6

U

Uber, 40

The Unbearable Lightness of Being (Kundera), 19

Uncertainty: free market consumer culture as hating, 1, 2, 3, 12; how mystery creates a space for surprise and, 12–13. *See also* Predictability

Underclass, 33–34

Universities: class warfare driven by the corporation of, 38; consequences of the competition driven by schools and, 32–33

University of Kansas, 38

Urban life: Cain's broken covenant and establishment of first city, 30; loss of the community due to nature of, 30–31

Usury as good business, 23

V

Vernacular language, 25, 50, 90–91

Violence: as expression of empire and class distinctions, 42; of parentless children, 42–43

Visitation Order of nuns, 72

Vulnerable: anger against food stamps and those "poor people," 35; corporate interest in staying blind to the needs of the, 38–39; covenant to see the gifts of the, 57; duty to protect the, 34–35; market ideology on the "undeserving" state of the, 39; the U.S. population of the, 34

W

Waiting lines, 65

Way of the Torah, 10

Wealth: class warfare's relationship to distribution of, 34–35; consumer market's un-productive, 41–42; covenantal or distributive justice and distribution of the community, 75; the emotional and spiritual question of how to use, 24. *See also* Money; Poverty

Wealthy man story, 14–15

Wholeness, 10

Wilderness: grief as communal practice recognizing making the choice of, 20; the Israelites' wish for safety while in the, 31, 81; neighborliness in the Old Testament, 49, 57; neighborhood and neighborliness as unexplored modern, 16; Old Testament metaphor of, 15–16

Williams, Roger, 48

Wills, Garry, 48

Winthrop, John, 48

Women's Movement, 82–83

Y

Yousuf, Hibah, 29